7 Secrets of Highly Successful Kids

Peter Kuitenbrouwer

Lobster Press ™

7 Secrets of Highly Successful Kids
Text © 2006 Peter Kuitenbrouwer
Illustrations © 2001 Lobster Press™

2nd Edition Published in 2006 by Lobster Press™
1620 Sherbrooke Street West, Suites C & D
Montréal, Québec H3H 1C9
Tel. (514) 904-1100 • Fax (514) 904-1101 • www.lobsterpress.com

Publisher: Alison Fripp
Editors: Alison Fripp & Meghan Nolan
Editorial Assistant: Morgan Dambergs
Illustrations: Helen Flook
Graphic Design & Production: Tammy Desnoyers

We acknowledge the financial support of the Government of Canada through the Book Publishing
Industry Development Program (BPIDP) for our publishing activities.

We acknowledge the support of
the Canada Council for the Arts
for our publishing program.

The Canada Council | Le Conseil des Arts
for the Arts | du Canada

Library and Archives Canada Cataloguing in Publication

Kuitenbrouwer, Peter, 1962-
    7 secrets of highly successful kids / Peter Kuitenbrouwer. -- New ed.

(Millennium generation series)
ISBN-13: 978-1-897073-41-4 / ISBN-10: 1-897073-41-0

    1. Success--Psychological aspects--Juvenile literature. 2. Self-actualization (Psychology)--
Juvenile literature. I. Title. II. Title: Seven secrets of highly successful kids. III. Series.

BF723.S77K84 2006   j158.1'083'4   C2005-907809-X

Printed and bound in Canada.

To Mimi, Tallulah and Frits
– Peter Kuitenbrouwer

Table of Contents

Foreword

by **Miriam McDonald**
of *Degrassi: The Next Generation*

From a very young age, I have been driven to succeed. This quality first truly presented itself when I was valedictorian. At age four. When I graduated from preschool.

As a "little sister," I naturally developed the need to stand out at a young age. My sister and I often vied for our parents' attention, and through this "competition," I learned early on how to be the "winner" and the "loser."

I much preferred to win (as many do!), and I paid careful attention to the tactics that were necessary to achieve my goals.

As I grew up, my goals began to change. At first, I wanted my parents to value me as much as I knew they valued my sister, which was not difficult to achieve, as my parents have always been loving and supportive. When I started school, I wanted to be smart, so I asked lots of questions. When I started swimming, I wanted to be fast, so I trained. When I started dancing, I wanted to be watched, so I performed. When I started acting, I wanted to make people laugh, so I laughed at myself. I also wanted to make people cry, so I didn't shy away from emotion. I have learned that I am driven by reaction. And whether someone reacts to what I do with compliments or with criticism, I use the response as a tool.

From my experiences, I have learned that making a mistake or falling flat on my face simply presents an opportunity to change and improve. I have carried that lesson with me, and it has been the force that propels me to stick with things, even when the going gets tough.

Some of my greatest successes have ultimately been some of my greatest challenges, which has made the triumphs much sweeter in the end. Hearing "No" sets off an alarm in my head that drives me, and makes me even more determined to succeed.

In fact, at age eleven, I was turned down by the first agent I ever met. After that rejection, I got on the phone with an acting coach and set up a session with him the next week. I refused to take no for an answer, and after a month of training, I returned to the same agent, and he signed me on the spot.

The first audition he sent me on was for a little show called "Degrassi: The Next Generation." I was cast as Emma Nelson.

I recently wrapped up my fifth season on the show.

My personal keys to success are determination, passion, and belief in myself. This combination is potent, and whether it leads to success or failure, it sure nurtures a fighting spirit!

In my eighteen years, I have been dealt my share of blows, but each time I'm knocked down, I simply pick myself up and try again with a little more wisdom in my back pocket.

I will never give up on something that I truly desire, no matter how unattainable it may seem at first. I've learned that each attempt gets you closer to your goal, and you can learn so much by just trying.

Success is not something you fall upon; it is something you earn. For this reason, I believe that success can be had by anyone who is willing to try.

Acknowledgements

So many people have helped me find the kids in this book: friends, family, co-workers, parents and coaches, teachers, and school board staff.

First of all, thank you to Sarah Murdoch at the *National Post* and Jaimie Hubbard, who had the original idea for the article that inspired this project. Also at the paper, thank you to Doug Kelly, John Racovali, and Rob Roberts for their support.

Thank you to Mimi Maxwell, my beautiful wife, who has helped me six ways past Sunday, and to Tallulah and Frits Kuitenbrouwer, our children, for their patience and love.

Thank you to all the kids and their family members who appear in these stories. You have let me into your lives in a way that warms my heart.

Thank you to my sisters, Sylvia van Oort, Noelle MacFarlane, and Marie-Josée Sheeks; and my niece, Linda van Oort, who helped me locate kids.

Thank you to my mom for helping me to be a successful kid, and to Michael Mouland: my agent, camping buddy, and true friend.

Also thank you to Gayle Akler, Pia Bouman, Desmond Brown, Catherine Buckie, Ian Cameron, Hamelin Grange, Leslie Hetherington, Colette Lelièvre, Marie-Claude Lortie, Scott and Patty Mason, Sherri Maxwell, Kimberly Noble, Dan Pellerin, Joanne Pierre, Louise Poulin, Stuart Solway, Emmanuelle Racine-Gariépy, Joan Walters, Dan Westell, Linda Wilson at the Winnipeg School Board, Gerry Donahue of The

Hockey Institute, Industry Canada's First Nations SchoolNet, and Treeda Smith from the Richmond District School Board.

I'd also like to thank Alison Fripp for having the vision to publish this book. I wish, finally, to acknowledge the patience of Kim Bourgeois and Meghan Nolan, my editors at Lobster Press, who shaped my words into these stories. I whined a lot but it's actually been fun.

Introduction

The kids are all right. And I am overjoyed to report it.

Let me give you a bit of history. I began this project six years ago as a newspaper article. My editor at the *National Post* asked me to interview kids and find out what tools they used to succeed in school. Now I must confess, I was never an amazing student – at least not in the narrow classroom sense of the word. I succeed now, as I did then, by busting out and trying new things. The work I did on the student newspaper in school, or stacking firewood on the farm where I grew up, or reading *Narnia* books, was just as important as my studies. I think we should measure kids by how well they tackle many different challenges: ski, swim, ride a horse, wash the dishes, get along with their friends, jump off a cliff into the lake (see page 103), do magic tricks, or sing a song.

So I set off to look for kids I believed to be successful. And I asked them their secrets. It wasn't easy. Like most journalists, I am used to interviewing adults. I had to work a bit harder to get kids to open up. But they talked, I scribbled it down, and in 2001, their stories and their secrets became the first edition of this book. It was all tremendous fun.

Five years later, those books are all sold. So we decided to put together a new edition. I dug the index cards out of the file box that's been sitting on my desk all these years, and wrote to the kids, to see how they were. I admit, I was a bit worried. What if they were all failures, unhappy, depressed, miserable? A lot can happen in five years, so I was a bit nervous about what I might learn. But lo and behold, the secrets worked! The kids are all right! Sure, they've had their ups and downs. Sam Friedman wrote to me: "I had a couple of jobs, but I got fired from both of them – don't know if you want that." But even getting fired, I think, can be a good thing. To see what I mean, read the seven updates – one per secret – that we include in this new edition.

Of course, the kids had changed. Graeme Moore, the tiny hockey player, at fourteen is now almost as tall as I am. David Armstrong, a pudgy little magician when I first met him, is on the rowing team; at fifteen, he's lanky and strong. When I went to his house he invited me to the kitchen for coffee. "Is a latte okay?" he asked, busying himself with the steamer. Cassie McPhee, a sweet twelve-year-old, is now a teen with a job and fake nails. John MacDonald is in university. Some are dating, and almost all have cell phones. But I am happy to report that in one key area these young people have not changed – they are still living by their secrets. This proves the key message from this book: the foundation you lay down in middle childhood, for overcoming odds, will serve you well throughout life.

The kids, of course, cannot succeed alone. The eighth secret, the one no child can do without, is support from their parents. When I went back to see young Graeme, I watched as his mother, Carla, piled copious amounts of soup, crackers, cheese and water in front of him. That was just an after-school snack! And both Carla and Glen, Graeme's father, are there to drive him to his hockey practices and games. As a parent, I've learned that support doesn't mean telling a kid what to do. I started

Tallulah, our daughter, in hockey skates. When she announced "I want white skates," I found her white skates. That makes Tallulah the exact opposite of young Deborah Conway in the book, who asked for black skates when her parents bought her white ones. When Tallulah announced she wished to switch from ballet to national dance, we supported her. The stories in this book prove that, when parents let their kids choose which quest or passion they want to pursue – within the parents' budget and boundaries, of course – kids love to sparkle, shine and succeed.

So enjoy this book. Then go out there and find your own personal success. And while you're doing so, for goodness sake, have a good time!

1 Choose a Good Role Model

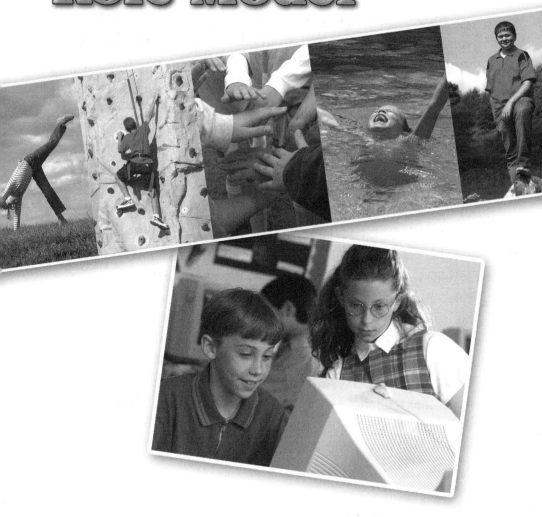

Laquisha Davis, age 12

On the day that Jeannie Boisineau moved into a century-old brick house in the downtown of a big southeastern city, her doorbell rang. "I went downstairs and there was this little third-grader at the door, with a book under her arm, *Are You My Mother?* by P.D. Eastman. She said, 'You need me to read to you.' " The impromptu visitor was Laquisha Davis, a neighbor from two doors down, who wanted to welcome the newcomer to her street.

"We sat on the step and she read the book," Jeannie recalls. "The next day there was a letter in my mailbox. She had copied out the book on paper, with little drawings in the margins, and signed it, 'Your friend, Laquisha.' "

Thus was born a beautiful friendship between Jeannie, a casting agent in the movie industry, and Laquisha, a girl brimming with talent and confidence, who has thrived by choosing good role models. "She has an extraordinary amount of discipline," says Jeannie, who later asked Laquisha to be the flower girl at her wedding. "And a lot of will beyond her years." Laquisha has had to overcome a great deal in order to succeed. Her grade school, Chimborazo Elementary, was founded 150 years ago, after the U.S. Civil War, to educate the children of freed slaves. Today, just as was true back then, the students are all African American, and are among the poorest in town. Many of the kids have just one parent at home. Few can afford to bring or buy food; most depend on government funding for lunch.

Laquisha's own father left when she was small. Today she and her two sisters, Bemontrice, who is ten, and Fianiqua, who is seven, live with their mother and their grandparents. They don't have much: last year, Laquisha qualified to participate in the People to People International exchange program, but her family couldn't afford to send her. Still, Laquisha has one key asset: a great number of excellent role models, starting with her family.

Laquisha's family provides a good example of hard work and determination. Her grandmother, Loretta Williams, drives a shuttle van for residents of an seniors' home. Laquisha's grandfather is a retired carpenter who still works on construction sites, and who is also single-handedly renovating the family home. The third role model is Laquisha's mother, Latrēss, who works in the banquet hall at a local hotel. (On a recent night, Latrēss worked until midnight, then returned to work at five o'clock the next morning).

"Her grandparents were very, very instrumental in Laquisha's education," says her fourth-grade teacher, Valencia Glasper-Thomas. "She came in eager, ready to work, ready to learn. She is very pleasant and very sweet." Adds Jeannie, "Her mom and her grandparents are always present, always interested, and they hold their kids to a very high standard."

Another good role model for Laquisha has been Cheryl Burke, the principal at Chimborazo. When Ms. Burke arrived in 1996, grades at the school were in the single digits. She brought in blue and white school uniforms, and prowled the neighborhood, "crying and begging" for parents to get involved.

Gradually the school began to improve, and Laquisha became a role model for that new culture of success. She got on the honor role in kindergarten, and stayed there. In fourth grade, she danced in a program of the city ballet to honor the Wright Brothers. Then in fifth grade, Laquisha discovered another love: painting.

"I just wanted to do art because my art teacher had encouraged me to join her art club," says Laquisha. She uses pencils, color pencils, pastels and markers. "We drew paintings like Georgia O'Keefe," she says. Her painting of flowers hangs today in the principal's office. "My art teacher told me it was a fantastic job, so she asked me to do another one." The second painting made it to an art fair in an historic part of town. Then Laquisha sold it to her friend Jeannie for twenty-five dollars.

When Laquisha was eleven, Jeannie nominated her for "16 under 16," a local newspaper's annual survey of talented kids. Laquisha's face beams from a photograph in the paper. Her arms are loaded with trophies. Then the superintendent of schools gave Laquisha one more award, as the most outstanding student in the city.

The key message from Jeannie and all of Laquisha's other role models is that Laquisha can achieve anything she sets her mind to. Jeannie wants her young friend to be president of the United States, but Laquisha, true to her confident self, has other plans. "It's too much work," she says of the presidency. "I want to be a pediatrician because I'll get to help little kids."

After fifth grade, Laquisha moved on to middle school. The closest school was not up to her standards, so she switched to another school, farther away. She gets there by school bus. These days she gets more homework, she says, but she is keeping her grades up.

In order to succeed, sometimes Laquisha has to make tough choices. She plays on the basketball team at the recreation center, and the team has an impressive winning streak. But sometimes, she says, she chooses school over sports. "I have to have my school work done before I do anything else like basketball or soccer. If I need more help with Spanish, I stay back for help from my teacher, and I don't go to basketball practice."

Having benefited from wonderful role models, Laquisha knows she must be a good role model herself. At home she cleans her room, washes the dishes and, she says, "Every now and then I sweep the floor." She also helps with the homework of her little sisters. The other night, she spent half an hour helping Bemontrice with fifth grade math: converting fractions into decimals.

"Sometimes I get frustrated, and she gets mad, because I know that she doesn't know. So I write down the answers and then I erase them and she does them on her own."

Recently for history class, Laquisha read the Laura Ingalls Wilder book, *Little House on the Prairie*. Like Laquisha, the family in that story doesn't have much. But, as Laquisha points out, they have the one thing that counts the most, just like Laquisha's own family.

"They all love each other," she says.

Yohance Francis Parsons, age 7

On a cold Sunday in March, Yohance Parsons arrives at his aunt Vivine's suburban house at three o'clock sharp. He's just come from Catholic Mass, and is wearing a silver double-breasted suit with a purple shirt and tie. He disappears for a few moments, then pops back out, wearing track pants and a green soccer jersey. He picks up his djembe, a drum made of goatskin stretched over a carved tree trunk.

The furniture in the living room is pushed to the sides. Yohance takes his station between his fifteen-year-old cousin, Kemar Scarlett, and an eleven-year-old fellow musician, Marcus Connell. "Thump! Thump! Thump!" The beat starts up. Kemar, in a black sweatshirt and Nike track pants, hits his drum confidently, with relaxed concentration. His pose makes it clear: he is the leader. Two girls—Kyesha Francis, age fourteen, and Shaleeka Scarlett, age eleven—plunge, jump, and sway to the beat. "Dance or Die," reads Kyesha's T-shirt.

This is the weekly rehearsal of the Ngoma drum and dance ensemble. ("Ngoma" is the Swahili word for both drum and dance.) The performers may be young, but they are very successful. Since forming in 1995, the ensemble has taken the stage at dozens of galas, celebrations, award shows, and festivals, treating crowds to African rhythms woven with calypso, reggae, and hip hop. According to Vivine, Yohance's aunt and the troupe's dance teacher, this recognition helps build the kids' self-esteem. "It reinforces a lot of stuff in the children even if they don't realize it or admit it," she shouts over the pounding of the drums.

Yohance, the youngest member of the group by far, is almost businesslike in explaining why he drums with the group. "I want to be an R&B singer," he says. "First I want to drum to get my music skills up."

For Yohance, whose parents are no longer together, drumming has been so much more than just musical training. It has been a constant in his life, something to look forward to. It's a warm weekly family gathering. His mom, Yvonne, dances and laughs with her sisters, the children play together, and everyone shares a big meal.

Most of all, Yohance cherishes the time spent with his big cousin Kemar, his mentor, friend, and role model. When Yohance speaks of Kemar, it is with reverence. "He's kinda like my brother," Yohance says, his eyes sparkling from behind wire-rimmed glasses. "I always wanted to be a good drummer like him—a master drummer. It takes skills to get to where he is."

Yohance is no stranger to drumming himself, having given his first unscheduled performance at age two. It was a sunny July afternoon, and he was on stage with his mother's African drum and dance troupe at a jazz festival. Yohance had attended all the troupe's rehearsals, and learned to drum as he learned to walk, though no one paid much attention. Then, that summer afternoon, he stole the limelight.

Sitting on a green plastic lawn chair so he could reach the drum, a baseball cap tipped backwards on his tiny head, he started to play. "He got on the drum and he just started soloing," his mother recalls. "The rest of the group brought the sound down. I was just blown away. And so of course tears were running down my face: 'That's my baby! He can play!'"

As he grows, Yohance takes on new challenges: in addition to drumming, he takes piano lessons, and recently won first prize in a regional music competition. He also studies martial arts two nights a week. Still, music is Yohance's first love. He is in awe of Kemar, who has rigged up his room as a recording studio. Kemar has a micro-phone and a computer program that allows him to build his own multi-track recordings.

Best of all for Yohance is when Kemar takes him along to his friends' houses, treating him with respect. "His friends know me," says Yohance. "We walk over, have fun, and we drum, too, playing little pieces on buckets or sometimes on the table. His friends just try and play along."

Kemar is also a patient teacher. At this week's rehearsal, he is continuing to teach the group a song he learned last month during four weeks of study in Guinea, West Africa. Kemar stops drumming in the middle of a song and places his hand on Yohance's drum. Yohance stops. Then Kemar drums a refrain, and the song continues. Later, I ask Kemar why he stopped Yohance halfway through the song. "He made a mistake with his part," Kemar explains. "So I played his part for a moment, to show him how it is done."

While Yvonne is glad that Yohance has a positive role model, she cautions her son not to idolize his cousin too much. "Yohance idolizes Kemar, and he also idolized Michael Jackson in his younger days," she says. "I tell him, 'You can identify with another youngster, but you have to develop your own identity. You have to identify what you love.' "

Yohance may find his identity as he gets the opportunity to be a mentor himself. And that chance is coming up. At the height of the Sunday rehearsal, Talib, Yohance's ten-month-old cousin, crawls fearlessly across the living room floor. He weaves his way through the dancing girls and reaches the boys on their drums. The tiny baby pulls himself up and begins to hit on a drum, learning to play the same way that Yohance did.

"When Talib is bigger," Yvonne tells her son, "you can show him the ropes."

Update

Yohance Francis Parsons, *now* age 12

Saturday evening, a week before Christmas, and the community center is full of kids. They sit at tables in the gym, each decorated with a little Christmas tree draped in candy canes. Balloons and streamers hang from the cement walls. The kids are about to feast on turkey, curried goat, jerk chicken and sweet potato pudding. But first, the Ngoma Drum and Dance Ensemble performs. Five members of the drum group arrive, in matching purple tie-dyed T-shirts and white do-rags. At the front, standing tall and pounding his djembe is Yohance Francis Parsons, age twelve.

Five years ago, Yohance was a junior member of the group. Today he is clearly a leader. As the group bangs out rhythms, filling the gym with African holiday cheer, even the older, tougher-looking youths turn to look and listen.

Life is rough around here. Kids often turn to guns, drugs and crime – a lifestyle glorified in a lot of rap music. This drum group offers a positive alternative: music from the roots of African heritage, which makes people feel good. Drumming for Yohance is a constructive outlet. In addition to performing, he teaches drumming workshops. Having chosen good role models when he was younger, he is now a positive role model himself. "The lessons give kids an opportunity to get off the streets," he says. "They don't turn to guns or drugs or whatever. So when we teach, it makes us feel like we're doing something positive." Yohance also earns money teaching: five dollars for every half hour drumming class he gives. At the same time, the group gives him a sense of belonging. "Ngoma is like family," he says.

Now the group is raising money to go to Ghana in Africa next summer, to adopt a school, conduct workshops and help in community-building. "I've never been to Africa so it's a privilege to be able to go," Yohance says.

Yohance stays busy – and has fun. He plays basketball on a team at the community center, but music remains his main focus. He has appeared on several television shows with the drum group. He toured North America with a children's choir, and has joined a steel pan group called Pan Fantasy. In addition, he is playing alto saxophone at school.

And he is still sticking to his secret: choosing good role models. His elder cousin, Kemar, left the drum group; Yohance now seeks to be like top-notch African drummers with whom he trains when he has a chance.

"These guys are more like role models to me since Kemar left," he says. "They're master drummers, among the best, so I try to mimic what they do."

Camille Boudreau, age 12

Every school morning, Camille arrives before eight at the door of the kindergarten at École Bois-Joli, a French school in a port city on the East Coast, and waits in the hall. It is not long before pandemonium strikes. Here they come, the five-year-olds, skittling around, bundled for winter. Camille helps them take off their snowsuits, boots, hats, scarves, and mittens. She reminds the children to arrange their winter clothes in their cubbies and put on their shoes. She helps them tie their laces, then leads them into the classroom to read and draw.

At a quarter past nine Camille says goodbye, and goes off to her own class. "She is so patient," Sophie De Jong, the kindergarten teacher, says of Camille. "Sometimes I'm exhausted and I feel like just ordering the kids around. But if a boy forgets to hang up his coat, Camille will just say, 'Are you forgetting something?' And he'll say, 'Oh yeah, my coat.' And then Camille will say, 'Good, let's go tell Mrs. Sophie how good you were.' "

This is Camille's second year volunteering in Sophie's class. This year she is there every morning, helping out. Her commitment to volunteer work has the whole school in awe.

"We see kids who are great musicians and great artists," says the principal, Louise Poulin. "But the fact that she gives back to the community like this, that's amazing. She plunges into that crazy brouhaha in the morning with those little kids. It's a thankless job. She has a wonderful personality."

Asked why she goes to the kindergarten every morning when most kids her age are enjoying an extra hour of sleep, Camille says, "Well, that's easy. I really like to be with the kids. Plus I want to be a teacher, and I know this will help me later when I try to get a job."

It's not just the kids, though. What keeps Camille coming back is the special bond she shares with Sophie, whom Camille has known since she was two. Sophie was Camille's babysitter and longtime ballet instructor. The two have become fast friends. And now that Sophie is a kindergarten teacher, Camille wants to be just like her. Sophie is Camille's biggest role model.

When Sophie was sixteen she started a ballet school called "Les Petits Ballets." Camille was her first student. Sophie continued teaching ballet all through university, using the money to pay for her studies. Now, Camille wants to copy that idea—reopen the ballet school with her ballet friend Selina, and use the money to pay for their studies.

Camille likes having a long-term goal. It gives her something to look forward to. In the meantime, her volunteer work in Sophie's kindergarten gives her the chance to practice her teaching skills. Both Sophie and Camille benefit from Camille's help. Camille gets a sense of purpose, belonging, and satisfaction. And

Sophie gets a helper, friend, and source of inspiration. "For me," says Sophie, "Camille is the little sister I never had. I can't wait to have children so that Camille can babysit."

Camille chooses good role models in general. She admires her parents, who, like Sophie, are also teachers. Camille has always known that she wanted to follow in her parents' footsteps. At age five, Camille sat her three-year-old sister, Jasmine, down on the floor and began teaching her how to read and write. Now she teaches reading at the kindergarten, and makes tapes of herself reading kids' books, so that the children can work on their reading at home.

For Valentine's Day, Camille used her computer to create a little personalized card (the kind kids can color in themselves) for each of the children in Sophie's class. She came in early, and put a card at each child's place. "The other teachers in the school say, 'We want a Camille,' " says Sophie. "They think they can go buy one at the store."

Camille gets another form of fulfillment from her volunteer work: the kids adore her. When the announcements come over the public address in the morning, the children in Sophie's class always become very quiet and listen very intently to hear whether the principal will announce that Camille Boudreau has won another prize. "They want to hear the name of Camille," says Sophie. "She's their personal hero."

And Camille has won lots of prizes. She won both the public speaking and top writing awards for her school and region; her science project won first place for research at her school; and in spelling, she won top honors for her school and region, and then flew to the national championships, where she took a top prize.

Camille loves to win awards, but the affection of her tiny kindergarten friends is what really warms her heart. "Yesterday a little boy named Bradley took a little homemade flower from his knapsack and gave it to me," Camille says. "I know that they appreciate that I am helping." Having good mentors—her parents and Sophie—has helped Camille to become a positive role model herself.

Rosalie Bigras, age 9

When Rosalie Bigras walked into the recording studio with her uncle Dan, she could not have dreamed of the strange world she was about to enter. Dan Bigras, a pop singer in Quebec, Canada, was producing an album to celebrate the Millennium. He asked Rosalie, who was seven at the time, to sing a duet with him. "He came to pick me up at school at three o'clock and we recorded a cassette," she recalls. "He told me the key to sing it in, and I did it in two takes."

The song, a tearjerker in which a father asks his daughter what the future might bring, made a splash. Journalists mobbed Rosalie at the album launch, and offers poured in from television shows. Everyone, it seems, wanted to make her a star.

"The night I went on one talk show, my uncle said, 'Don't be afraid, there are only 850,000 people watching you,' " Rosalie recalls. "And I was like, 'Uggggh!' The next day at school everyone said 'I saw you on TV on the weekend,' and 'Can I have your autograph?' It makes you feel all big, but in fact you're real small."

Journalists kept asking Rosalie whether she plans a career as a singer. "I don't know," she answered. "It's far away in the future. My uncle plays three instruments and sings. It's a lot of work to get there." Rosalie tasted the big time. Now, she is happy to be back in the life of a regular third grader, tobogganing with her elder sister on the weekends.

Rosalie's uncle Dan has been a good role model: he is living proof that success comes through hard work. He noticed Rosalie's musical talent and nurtured it. But he has also guided her to take it slow, and develop in her own good time — not focus on stardom at the expense of childhood.

Rosalie showed an early love of music. "When she was at daycare, she'd learn the songs and come home and sing and sing until we were fed up," says Nathalie, her mother. In grade one, thanks to a top mark on a music test, Rosalie became one of ninety kids from sixty schools given the chance to enroll at a special public school for gifted musicians. But when she went with her mom to check out the school, Rosalie wasn't sure that she wanted to transfer. "We went into a classroom and there were thirty kids playing the violin," she recalls. "It was intimidating. It was stressful. I was afraid."

Nonetheless, Rosalie gathered all her courage and enrolled. As a fresh-faced second grader, she found the school every bit as challenging as she had feared. "In the regular school she was one of the top students," says her mother. "She was used to being the one to yell the answer. But at this school, fifteen kids were yelling the answer. It was tough on her ego."

The school requires the students to cover the same reading, writing, and math as other schools in a lot less time. That way, they can devote time to music. The homework gets laid on pretty thick, and anybody who flunks gets kicked out.

That Christmas, Rosalie came within a hair's breadth of dropping out, but she stuck with it. Of twenty-seven kids in her grade two class, only eighteen came back for grade three. Rosalie, who plays violin and flute, was one of them. "I listen a lot at school so it's not tough for me," she says. As for the music, she says she likes the flute best. "When you know how to play, you have all the fingerings in your head."

For years, Rosalie's famous uncle Dan lived in the house next door. She cherishes memories of fun, silly times: fights for the TV remote that turned into tickling sessions between Rosalie, her uncle, and his little son. "My uncle is nice, he's funny, and he is a scoundrel," she says.

Dan often heard his niece singing at his house and at family gatherings, so he knew she'd be right for his album, though he didn't know quite how perfect she'd be. "I gave her the lyric sheet and she sang it a few times and memorized it," he recalls. "I think that, at age seven, it was easier for her to memorize the words than to read them. Then she sang into the mike and it was just perfect. Her pitch and her timing were bang on. All the other artists and engineers fell on their butts. They couldn't believe it. She's a natural."

In the studio, Rosalie got so excited that she started to swing, and her mouth strayed from the microphone. Her uncle went behind her and held her hips to the chair so the microphone could capture her voice. Later on live TV, Rosalie had memorized the words so well she sang flawlessly, while her uncle flubbed it and sang the last stanza at the start. "My uncle messed up," she remembers. "I told him, and he told everybody, and we all laughed."

Rosalie's uncle sensed that putting a child into the spotlight can be dangerous. "At the record launch I had forgotten a bit that she was a kid. The media were all after Rosalie. At one point I had to call off the dogs, to protect her, and I know when she went home that night, she cried."

Rosalie's mom and her uncle agree: they don't want her to become a child star and miss out on being a kid. After a few TV shows, her mom pulled the plug. Today, Dan says he's happy if he's transmitted to his niece the will to do things with passion. He doesn't want to steer her in any particular direction.

"If she has a passion to sell toothbrushes, then let her sell toothbrushes," he says. "I had dreams and passions, and what I earned belongs to me. For it to be hers, we have to let her earn it. As adults we ask too much of our children."

2 Be Organized

Amy Strizic, age 9

It's Tuesday afternoon. I've been hanging out in the Strizic family's living room for about two hours, talking with Amy and her mother, Pat. Amy's been telling me about her life and her family's wide assortment of household pets. There's Jesse and Brook, the two Bouvier dogs; Jerry and Sidney, the chicadees; an aquarium full of fish (small catfish, neons, and balloon mollies); and Tom Thumb, the little turtle they rescued from the pool out back. Then, out of the blue, Amy does something that surprises me. She lifts her left arm and looks at her watch.

Now it's not often I see a nine-year-old check the time, but believe me, if you were Amy, you would check too. Since it's Spring Break, Amy doesn't have much in the way of homework. Still, all this sitting around and gabbing could make a fourth grader late for something. She does, after all, have a Pre-Elementary Ballet class at 5:30 p.m.

I catch up with Amy again the following Wednesday at the Pia Bouman School for Ballet & Creative Movement, in a wooden old church hall. It's half past four and the place is coming alive with a kind of creative chaos. Children's laughter echoes in big rooms with soaring ceilings, sunlight pours through tall windows, and the scuffed floorboards creak under the pitter-patter of little feet. Far away, someone plays a song on a battered old piano. It is time for Amy's modern dance class.

Meagan O'Shea, the teacher, arrives ten minutes late. She peels off her pants to reveal black leggings, takes off her socks, and plugs in the CD player. Before her, like tittering birds, stand five little girls, aged nine to eleven, in bare feet. One of them is Amy. Dressed in a navy body suit and black leggings, her long hair pulled back in a ponytail, her outfit is similar to those of the other girls.

But one detail makes Amy stand out: she's the only girl wearing a watch. It's her trusty Casio Illuminator, lime green, and she never takes it off. With all her activities, Amy needs to know the time.

Amy's schedule involves four dance classes every week. Mondays and Tuesdays, she has ballet at 5:30 p.m. Wednesdays, she takes modern dance at 4:30 p.m. and ballet at 6:30 p.m. On Thursdays, during lunch, her mom picks her up at school and Amy eats in the car on her way to a cello lesson. Later the same day, she has another cello lesson, followed by piano from 5:00 to 5:30 p.m.

Friday evenings, in winter, it's off to the ski hill. On Saturdays, she has ski lessons from 9:30 a.m. to 12:30 p.m., and from 1:30 p.m. to 3:30 p.m. Sunday mornings, she has more ski lessons. To top it all off, Amy is also part of a national reading club. So far this year she's read five of the club's fiction books and three non-fiction, and she's in the middle of another novel: *Sunwing*, by Kenneth Oppel. Whew! With a schedule like that, wouldn't you wear a watch?

Surprisingly, Amy's action-packed agenda doesn't phase her. The key, she says, is to not waste time. On weekdays, Amy gets up at quarter to seven. By half past seven, she is finished breakfast. Then she sits down at the piano and practices a couple of pieces of music before heading off to school. Arriving at school at twenty after eight, she heads to the library, to either borrow a new book or read a few pages before class begins.

In the evening, when she has completed her ballet or piano lessons, she sets the table or helps her mother with dinner. "When I've finished my chores, I pick up my book and read for awhile," she says.

She doesn't watch TV much, other than music videos and one favorite show. "It frees up a lot of time if you don't watch too much TV," says her mom. "It's amazing."

At eight-thirty or quarter to nine, Amy goes to bed. "The kids in my class go to bed at nine or ten," she says. "But I'm sure you've heard that expression, 'Early to bed, early to rise, makes a man healthy, wealthy, and wise'? It gives you a lot of sleep so you're not really tired, so it's easy for you to get up in the morning."

Things slow down a bit in the summers, though Amy does spend an action-packed month at girls' camp. There in the wilderness park, a four-hour drive from her home, she makes pottery, weaves, wind-surfs, rides horses, and plays tennis and basketball.

Even at camp, Amy takes pride in being prompt for all her

activities. "Last year one time it rained a lot and the path flooded," she recalls. "I was one of only two girls who showed up on time for pottery class."

As well as being on time, Amy likes to be fully focused. Back in the modern dance class, the girls are learning a new step. "One, two, close circle, arms, over, up, side, tendu, stretch, over, circle, and around," Meagan calls, leading the girls across the floor. Moving together, Amy and her best friend, Stephanie, stretch out their arms like wings. They move with a grace that sets them apart from the others.

At half past five, the class is over. Amy and Stephanie have an hour before their next class. This hour is sacred—a chance to unwind and eat a healthy (well, mostly healthy) meal. She and Stephanie recall fondly the times they spent in the dance school kitchen last year, building a fort out of blankets draped over the table. "Oh and remember the time we built a fort through the whole room and we got in trouble?" Stephanie says.

Actually, Pia Bouman, the owner of the school, didn't mind at all. "Some ten-year-olds are bursting to hit the scene," she says. "Amy is still a child, building tents."

Yes, but only in her down time.

John MacDonald, age 12

It's a fine Tuesday morning during Spring Break. John MacDonald and his mother, Karen, get in the car and drive about forty-five minutes to the Microbiology building at the university campus downtown. They load up the car with a Bunsen burner, Petri dishes, sterile swabs, pipettes, bottles of brain heart infusion and agar (two nutrients that feed bacteria), and a portable incubator oven, all on loan from a professor John has befriended.

Add to this equipment a pound of hamburger meat that's been sitting in the open for six hours, a piece of formica, a marker, and a variety of cleaning products, and you have the basic components for John's entry into a regional science fair. The purpose of John's experiment is to test how well antibacterial soaps kill the bacteria found on countertops.

John is one busy kid. He attends a private school, where he faces the challenge of four quizzes and three tests a week. To keep up with the workload, he needs to do three or four hours of homework per night. Then there's his science project, which requires several weeks of preparation. Plus he's captain of his school basketball team (they stink, though John says it's not his fault). As if all this weren't enough, he also studies piano and clarinet, and skis on weekends.

Despite his hectic schedule, John seems happy and calm. The key, he says, is to plan ahead and maintain a balance between brain work and exercise. It's also important to recognize that you can't do everything. "There's no way I could get the marks that I get and join a basketball league," he says. "I'd leave at 6:30 p.m. to go to a game and get home at 9:00 p.m.—it just wouldn't work." (John's school basketball team practices right before or after classes, which meshes with his busy schedule.) As for hanging out with friends, he says, "You have to really plan ahead. If you know you're going to have a friend over on Sunday, you make sure to do an extra amount of homework on Friday night."

John's the only twelve-year-old I know with a planning diary, and it puts mine to shame. His allots thirteen lines for each school day, and just about every line is carefully filled in, in pencil, with homework assignments and reminders about quizzes, tests, and exams. When John completes a task, he checks it off in red pen; when he doesn't, he adds it in red to the following day's "to do" list.

"The first and most important study habit," says John, "is probably listening in class. It doesn't matter if you understand everything the first time as long as you hear it. When you have a test, study a few days before, but try not to go ballistic at the last minute. Plan and write down when all the tests are so you don't forget about one. As long as you keep up-to-date and don't let homework slide, you're okay. Once you get into the cycle of delay, major projects and tests come up, and you don't have time to be delaying like that."

He admits that staying focused is not always easy. "The worst is in June. You come home and you hear the boy down the street, and he's shooting hoops and you think, 'Boy, if I wasn't in private school I could be out there.' But then I remember that I chose to be in private school. It's all about choices that I have to make."

Two pages long, John's resumé lists awards in debating, public speaking, and athletics, as well as second prize in a national science fair. Last year, John entered the science fair with a box he designed with his father. A thermometer in a bowl of hot water placed inside the box allowed him to test the insulating powers of Styrofoam, fiberglass, and wood chips. "The box wasn't rocket science," says John. "It was all in the presentation."

Yet John got all the way to the national science fair, where he won a silver medal, two prizes totaling $800 in cash, and a $2,000 university scholarship. To top things off, he got to have his picture taken with Vince Carter, the basketball star.

To succeed at this level, John depends a lot on the help of his parents. They fire questions at him to prepare him for quizzes and exams, and brainstorm ideas with him for his projects. For this year's science fair, John first thought of designing a tap filter to cleanse water of a deadly strain of E. coli. "Problem is, it's highly dangerous," he explains. "Then my mom said, 'What about the bacteria in hamburger meat?' "

John and his parents have fun fooling around, too. John tells with laughter how he and his father took a side trail on the ski hill the other day and ended up dodging trees in four feet of powder.

"I don't want to give up skiing because that's my retreat from it all," John says. "When it's time to play, it's time to play, and you don't think about the mounds of paper on your desk that are crying out for your attention. And when you're working, you focus on that. It allows you to maintain order in your life, and certainly balance."

Update

John MacDonald, *now* age 18

Since I last saw John, he has proven that being organized has its rewards. Having graduated high school, he has set sail on a new adventure, to university. There, thanks to all the preparations he made in high school, he is having a great time.

John's high school career came to a dramatic end on a sweltering evening in June, when he took the stage in the auditorium at his private Catholic school. The room was packed with people, and so hot that the fire alarm kept going off.

John, though, was not rattled. He was the valedictorian of his graduating class, and he had a speech to give. "Napoleon said, 'Victory belongs to the persevering,'" John told the room. "Each and every one of the ninety-six graduates here tonight has persevered."

John, in fact, did a lot more than persevere. After seven years of a punishing schedule at private school (plus hobbies on the side, such as volunteering for the Catholic Church's World Youth Day) he graduated, third in his class, with awards for the top grade in both physics and chemistry. That success translated into scholarships for university, worth a total of $24,000 over four years.

I spoke to John in his dorm room at his university, in a small northeastern college town. He is now eighteen. The semester was ending and John had three exams looming: physics, chemistry and biology. He was studying eight or nine hours a day, but even so, he was in great spirits.

"I pretty much have the life of Riley now," he said happily. John was so focused during high school that now studying seems to come easier. Many people struggle in first semester of university, but John told me that for him, "School doesn't seem to take up as much time as it once did."

To the secret, "Be Organized," John now adds a corollary: "Don't try to succeed at too many things at once." "I can't even think back to how I did so many different things all at the same time, when I was twelve," he says.

Gone are the piano lessons and being captain of the basketball team. He has stripped his life down to four things: his girlfriend, studying, volunteering, and recreational sports.

As part of his volunteer work, John spends about fifteen hours a week finding corporate sponsors for a branch of the Room to Read charity, which raises money to build schools in the Third World. On top of doing good, the job teaches him how to network in the business world, he says.

When it's time to wind down, he uses sports such as basketball or lifting weights to relax and focus his mind. "Studying can be very aggravating," he says. "You have to take breaks and do something that doesn't involve your mind. Exercise is a good stress relief and a good break." Whereas in high school he played competitive basketball and raced on skis, now he just exercises for fun and for stress relief.

Not surprisingly, given that science project for which he won a prize way back when, John today is majoring in biology, though he's unsure of a career path. All he knows is that, as always, he is learning – and enjoying himself. "You can only really study well," he says, "if you take an interest in it." And with those parting words, John went back to his books.

Yanick Allwood, age 9

It's clear walking into the Allwood home that song is at the very center of the household. In a cage hanging in the entrance hall lives Nat, the green canary, named after singer Nat King Cole. Nearby flutter Chip and Chuck, the two budgies. All three birds chirp in joyous harmony. In the family room, an acoustic guitar is propped beside the couch. Then there's a spanking new Yamaha electric piano, a computer hooked up to huge speakers, and a hulking amplifier on the floor. And oh, yes, somewhere in the distance, there is a TV.

In the middle of all this is Yanick Allwood. Barely nine, he got his first big break this spring: he landed the role of young Simba in a production of Disney's *The Lion King*, and rehearsals begin soon. "I just can't wait to be king," says Yanick, a broad smile on his face.

Yanick gained his first exposure to music from his father, who learned to play guitar growing up in Jamaica. Filmore, who claims to have learned some bad attitudes as a child, strives to teach his kids to maintain a more positive outlook. "We don't emphasize 'can't' and 'I don't know,' " says Filmore. "We don't say, 'It is hard and I can't do it.' I grew up using these words and it hinders your progress. In this house, we say, 'It is challenging and I will accomplish it.' When you say 'I'll do it,' then you have to make a plan."

The family noticed Yanick's talent for music from a very early age. "I used to put on some earphones and push the wall like it was a tape recorder. Then I'd start singing, pretending I was in a recording studio," Yanick recalls. When Yanick was four, Filmore took him to meet his Seventh-Day Adventist church choir, where Yanick landed a solo part for a concert that was two weeks away. The pair went home and started practicing. Filmore taught Yanick the tune while Yanick's mom, Joyce, taught him the words. Yanick performed, without a hitch, to an audience of 400. News of his powerful, beautiful singing voice spread across the city. He sang in churches and school auditoriums, and at age seven, he released his first album: *Inspired*.

Yanick succeeds because he is talented, motivated, and passionate. But most of all, he is organized, and spends his time wisely. He doesn't watch much TV (although he does love old musicals and weekend cartoons), and follows a tight schedule, drawn up by his father. Four to five o'clock is homework, and five to six is supper. After supper, there is "quiet time," a period to sit and rest. Then the schedule varies: Mondays, Yannick and his brother have piano, and Wednesdays and Thursdays, they have voice lessons. Each boy must practice piano half an hour a night (there are two pianos in the home), and Yanick sets aside other time to rehearse for upcoming concerts.

Yanick sticks closely to his timetable. "When he comes home in the evening I don't have to ask, 'Do you have homework?'" his father says. "He automatically sits down at the kitchen table and starts to work." Yanick even likes to kill two birds with one stone: while he does his math and spelling, he sings to himself, going over melodies. "It's like music playing in the background," his father says. Yanick's method yields results: he recently brought home a report card with eight As and four Bs. He said, "Daddy, I want twelve As."

In singing, success involves practice, practice, and more practice. Before the four *Lion King* auditions, Yanick says he practiced for four weeks with Rashaan, his six-year-old brother. Rashaan played the voices of Scar, Nala, Zazu, and Mufasa, and helped Yanick with the singing. They practiced even while doing their chores, which include feeding the birds and fish, and cleaning the cages and aquariums. "He was the main person who helped me," Yanick says. "I feel lucky to have a brother."

Yanick sees performing as a contest. "To me every concert is like a competition," he says. "I think to myself, 'I can be better, I can get better marks than the person before me.' Whenever I sing for an audience and they stand up and applaud, it really makes me feel that I've done my best and accomplished a lot."

To win that acclaim, Yanick says he has to show up prepared. "I go through a warm-up session if my throat is sore. And I bring a water bottle with me. I am well bathed, well groomed, well dressed, and well rested," he says. "And well fed," pipes in his mother.

Still, it's not always easy. According to Yanick, some audiences are tough. "Sometimes I think they're bored or they've been nailed down to stay still," he says. And at times Yanick's schedule of public appearances exhausts his parents. Filmore and Joyce have to help select music, rehearse, plan routes, drive, buy clothing ...

Yet despite all the hard work and running around, you get the sense that Yanick loves to sing, and can't get enough of it. On top of his busy schedule, he has somehow found time to compose not one but two songs to celebrate Kindree Public School, which opened this year. He sits down at the keyboards, the tips of his toes barely reaching the floor, and begins to play.

"Everybody has a purpose to be here at Kindree," he sings. "Everybody has a purpose to be here now. Kindree is a place to be, and it's built for you and me. When you come here you will see that we work here in peace and harmony."

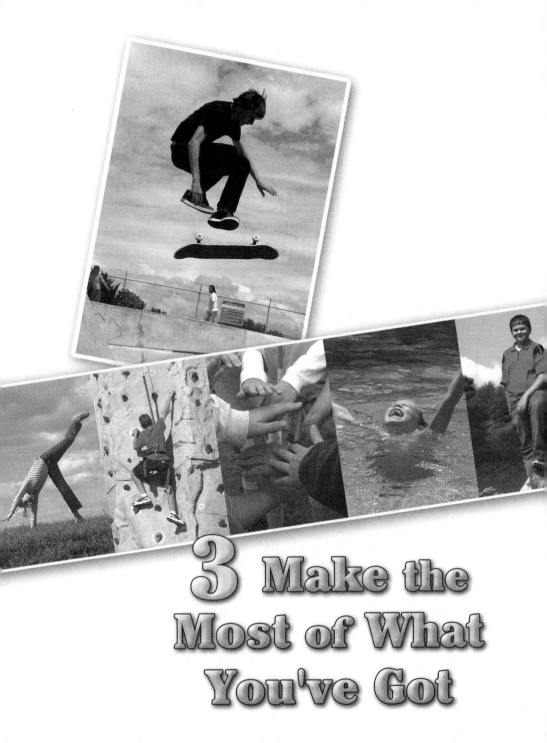

3 Make the Most of What You've Got

Sydney Kramer, age 12

"The Case of the Stolen Prom Dresses," the first book in the Cookie Dalmatian series, written by Sydney Amanda Kramer, stars Cookie Dalmatian, a New York City dog who likes to do two things: play football and solve mysteries. In the book, Cookie tracks down the thief who stole the prom dresses belonging to his girlfriend, Roxy, and her friends. Along the way, he meets Detective McBishon, a sheep dog who smokes a bubble pipe, and Syd Keeshond, a collie who works at the Hip Hop Helicopter CD store. According to the story, "The girl dogs loved him because he had soft spiked-up hair and rode a motor scooter."

It's a fast and funny book. My favorite part is Sydney's description of the villain, a thieving St. Bernard: "Alan S. was one of the most dangerous dogs in town, according to the police. He robbed other dogs and spanked puppies that weren't his."

There is just one difference between Sydney Kramer and most authors: when her first book came out, Sydney was eleven years old.

Sydney lives with her parents, Jackie and Marc Kramer, and her elder sister, Ariel, on the outskirts of a big eastern city. Her mom runs a service for business speakers, and her father, an author, has written five books about success in business.

Sydney has a learning disability, something her parents describe as "central auditory problems." She has to go to special classes to work on her reading comprehension. "She's better at learning from seeing than reading," explains her father. "School is a struggle for her and she has to work twice as hard." Adds her mother, "I think Sydney always felt a little out of the loop when it came to her peers, because of the learning issues."

But despite that challenge, Sydney has two big things going for her. The first is a very creative mind. "You could see that she had all these ideas running around in her head," says her fifth grade teacher, Pam Booraem of Uwchlan Hills Elementary School. At age nine, Sydney dreamed up an idea for a family restaurant called Boomerang, where a trolley on a track would transport diners to different rooms, each decorated in the theme of a vintage cartoon, such as *The Flintstones*, *The Jetsons* or *Jonny Quest*.

Sydney's second big advantage is her incredibly supportive family. Her father, Marc, had noticed that, because of her struggles with learning, Sydney sometimes didn't feel very good about herself, and was often shy and quiet at school. He figured out that Sydney needed something to improve her self-confidence. Seeing his daughter's creative energy, he reasoned that she would feel proud if she published a book, as he has done.

Just after she turned eleven, Sydney dreamed up Cookie Dalmatian. "I started telling my dad all these stories at dinner," she says. "Like Nancy Drew, Harry Potter, the Hardy Boys." Her father did what he does best: he wrote it all down. They began to work on a book together. "I would challenge her thinking about the chronology of the book, to help her with critical learning." Linda Stauffer, a local artist who had approached Sydney's dad for help with a business plan, contributed the illustrations, and three months later, the family self-published Sydney's first book, "The Case of the Stolen Prom Dresses."

All at once, Sydney's shyness disappeared. On her way to Hebrew school, she ran up to the rabbis to show them her new book. The local newspaper wrote a story about the book, and kids came up to her at school and asked for her autograph. And best of all, her teacher, Mrs. Booraem, asked her to read it to her fifth grade class.

"Doing presentations was not her favorite thing, but she got up and read the book to the class," recalls Mrs. Booraem. "It was good for Sydney to come out of her shell. She was just so proud of her book. And the book was really good. The students had millions of questions, because, you know, how often do they get to hear an author read, and it's one of their classmates? So it was a really neat experience for her."

These days, Sydney feels great about herself. "I'm like a mini Michelle Pfeiffer," she says. She certainly dresses the part of a movie star. She went through what her mom calls her "radical phase," where she wore red, blue, purple and black headbands, like a biker – color-coordinated, of course, with her outfits. She now sports long, sparkling earrings and bracelets with beads and funky little charms.

Today Sydney is very excited about her earning potential as

a budding author. "It's all about the Benjamins, baby," she says. Her allowance, ten dollars a week, just wasn't enough. "I took the money we would have given her in allowance and invested it in the book publishing," her father explains. Another family member built a website to sell the book. The first mystery sold about 100 copies, at twelve dollars each, across the United States and as far away as England and Panama. And now Sydney has a second Cookie Dalmatian book out: "The Diary of Ms. Jane French Bull."

Of each sale, Sydney donates one dollar to an arts center named for Katie Stauffer, the daughter of Cookie Dalmatian illustrator Linda Stauffer. Katie was killed in a car accident two years earlier.

Sydney has benefited from having a father who can mold her creativity into book form, as well as from the strong backing of both her parents. "Sydney has a very strong family," says her teacher. "Her parents were extremely supportive."

These days, Sydney is feeling more self-assured. "I think the attention she got from the book made her believe in herself, as in, 'Okay, so I'm a little different, but it's okay,'" says her mother.

Making the most of her creative mind and her supportive family – especially her father's skill in writing and publishing books – has taken Sydney from feeling shy to feeling self-assured. "It's something that Sydney and I can do together," says her father. "It builds up her self-esteem." It sure does: now, Sydney has set her sights on being a guest on "Oprah."

Chelsey MacDonald, age 11

Chelsey MacDonald lives in a small town, a ten hour drive from any city. Nestled in a valley out west, the town has a population of only 1,200. Soaring hills, thick with evergreens and poplar trees, circle the village, and clear mountain streams trickle down the hills into the valley.

The air here is clear and crisp. There's not much crime, but people regularly lose their cats to cougars and coyotes. There are plenty of black and brown bears around too, bold enough to steal plums from the trees in people's yards. Elk, moose, and white-tailed deer are also common sights.

The town itself boasts a couple of video stores, an elementary and a high school, a few motels and gas stations, a food shop, a sawmill, and a bank. "It's like, drive by and it's gone," says Chelsey's dad, John, who was born and raised here. The town does not have many of the things that city kids take for granted, such as malls, movie theatres, and clothing stores. If a kid from New York or Vancouver came to visit, they might look around and say, "Oh my God. What is there to do?"

Still, Chelsey's little town has one thing that would make plenty of city dwellers drool: a ski hill. It's three minutes from Chelsey's house, the powder is plentiful most years, and you can buy a season's pass for the price of a pair of shoes.

Chelsey, who was born here eleven years ago, didn't waste any time. By the age of three, she had already grasped a secret that many grown-ups never learn: make the most of what you've got. She clipped on her cousin's old skis, went up the ski hill, turned around, and came down.

According to Chelsey, her first time down the hill wasn't the biggest thrill. "This guy was behind me. I was wearing a harness with a rope on it, so if I was going into an area where I shouldn't, he would pull me back over," she recalls. But she gave it a fair shot and kept trying. As she improved, she quickly realized how much fun it could be: "At first I was thinking 'This is, like, hard and I won't be able to do it.' Then I eventually got off the harness thing and I got better and better and better."

Last year, Chelsey's ski team took the silver medal at a competition at a nearby hill. In the eight years since she started skiing, Chelsey has consistently ranked well at her own hill, too. She's placed first in three different age categories: seven and under, nine and under, and twelve and under. Not bad for an eleven-year-old, who, for seven years, competed wearing skis that were twice her age.

Winning requires a lot of work, though. When the snow builds up here, in early December, Chelsey practices five days a week. Tuesdays and Thursdays, she's with her team three hours per evening, and she practices six hours a day on Saturdays and Sundays. Wednesday nights, for a change of pace, she goes skiing with her girlfriends!

"She is the most outgoing person on the team," says Chelsey's twenty-year-old coach, Kirk Swchenko. "She's got an awesome attitude. She always comes into the lodge with her ski boots already on."

Making the most of what you've got is something Chelsey learns from her parents and community. People in her town generally don't have much money. Many of the jobs, such as logging, construction, and road work, are seasonal, which means Chelsey's father is occasionally out of work. What John and the others do have is time.

The community owns the ski hill, and both Chelsey's parents help to keep the hill running. Last year, Chelsey's father built an addition on the lodge, next to which he constructed an outdoor ice rink. Margaret, Chelsey's mother, lines up all the people that look after the kitchen on the hill.

Chelsey pitches in too: she does volunteer work, helping out with fundraisers at the daycare. And with her paper route, she saved up enough money to buy a new downhill ski suit— one another kid had owned but never worn. Chelsey doesn't let anything get in the way of her passion, though. While she enjoys having a bit of cash, when the snow starts to blow in the fall, she gladly hands her paper route over to her big sister.

As much as Chelsey loves to ski, like everyone, she enjoys a bit of variety. Being resourceful helps her to find lots of other fun stuff to do. In fact, watching her go almost makes you want to leave those city malls behind and move to her small town.

Monday and Friday nights, she practices curling with

her mom. At school, she plays on the basketball, volleyball, and softball teams. In the summer, when the ski hill is closed, she participates in a reading program at the library. She's also joined a recreational program, which takes her on fishing and kneeboarding expeditions. And then there are those lazy summer days when she just hangs out at the creek, floating lazily downstream on a big black innertube.

All in all, Chelsey has a good life. Maybe she doesn't get all the cool new stuff that some other kids have, but that doesn't seem to matter. She appreciates what she does have, and makes the most of it. As Chelsey has discovered, lots of things can be fun if you have the right attitude. She even has a good time volunteering at the daycare fundraisers.

"It's kind of fun," says Chelsey, summing up her philosophy, "more fun than staying at home."

Update

Chelsey MacDonald, *now* age 16

In January 2002, just a few months after I wrote about her, Chelsey MacDonald went to a ski race on a hill seven hours from home, and on a warm-up run, broke her leg.

"It was the first run of the day," she says. "It was really powdery and bumpy. There was a cataract thing. I went into a dip, hit down, and broke my leg. I managed to pop off my skis and climb about fifteen feet onto the flat part. I was laying there all by myself screaming for someone to find me. It was quite scary actually. A random skier came and saved me. Then I went to the hospital for surgery, and they forgot to give me painkillers. I woke up in the middle of the night, screaming." The following season, she says, she retired from ski racing.

Now here is a tough question: what do you do when your secret is, "Make the most of what you've got," and what you've got is a ski hill beside your house, and you retire from skiing? Answer: take up snowboarding (for fun) and move on. Which Chelsey, now sixteen, has done – now that she has gotten over her disappointment.

"It was sad that skiing was over," she says. When you're living the life of a ski racer and then it ends all of a sudden, Chelsey says, "it's like I can't do this, oh, I can't go there." But now she has let go of skiing, and has found plenty of other things to look forward to.

These days, in grade eleven, Chelsey is on the Principal's List, making her one of the highest ranking students at her school. She has made it to the championships three times with her softball team. She is working on becoming a lifeguard. She plays on a winning volleyball team. She has her driving learner's permit. She has learned first aid. She has a job in the deli at the local grocery store, prepping baked goods and cutting up lunch meat. Chelsey is also a student council member, and when we spoke she was organizing a school dance.

But here's the biggest excitement. Like Cassandra McPhee in Chapter Six, Chelsey is heading to Italy and France on a school trip next year. To raise money – about $3,000 per student – they are doing bottle drives, going door to door to collect empties. They also sold Christmas trees, and even wooden fencing, which they got from a kid whose father owns a sawmill.

"I can't wait to go to Europe," she says. "I've never even been on a plane." Chelsey is still making the most of what she's got. Turns out, though, that the most important thing in her life is not a ski hill in the back yard. It is her strong mind and healthy body, her energy and spunk, and she is making the most of that.

Antoine Asselin, age 11

On a Saturday afternoon in March, about fifty kids–mostly boys aged eleven to seventeen– are gathered at the Universe Skate Park, way out beyond the oil refineries on the outskirts of a big eastern city. An indoor skateboarding competition, the first of the season, is underway in this hulking cinderblock emporium. Antoine Asselin is perched at the lip of a ramp, six feet off the ground. Most of his skateboard juts over the edge, pointing into midair, the back of the board held to the ramp by Antoine's foot.

Antoine gazes off into the distance. Then he plunges, glides along the floor, climbs an incline, and jumps into the air. He lands without effort, as though his skateboard were an extension of his feet, and slides along a steel banister.

"Let's go, Antoine!" a spectator shouts, and other kids bang their boards against the railings in appreciation.

To a newcomer, this is a forbidding place. Grinding punk music blasts from the speakers, spray-painted scrawls are the only decor on the bare cement walls, and the kids in their running shoes, baggy pants, hooded sweatshirts, and helmets look vaguely menacing. The judge is a kid with a baseball cap turned backwards over died red hair. He has a stud through his eyebrow, a necklace of skulls, and a clipboard.

But watch! As Antoine swoops, glides, jumps, slides, and lands, the blaring music, graffiti, and ugly strip mall in distant suburbia disappear. All you see is the beauty of a young man among his peers, performing at the height of his game, proud and happy.

And on the balcony, his mom, Danielle (one of only three people in the building over the age of thirty), places two fingers of her right hand in her mouth and blows a piercing blast of approval that would make a cowboy proud.

"The first time I went into a skateboarding park," says Danielle, "I was not reassured. It's a pretty heavy culture, dark, noisy, scary. I had to go there many times, listen to the kids and watch them. I realized little by little that there are nice values in this milieu. They help each other. All the social classes are there. There are a lot of good people, and they respect each other. The older kids help the younger kids." "We're all friends," says Antoine.

When he was seven, Antoine found a skateboard in a garage at his mom's friend's house. He tried it out. Then his mom bought him his first board for Christmas, a clunky 'Toys "R" Us' job. It wasn't easy at first. "I showed up in pants that were too wide and too short, with the wrong kind of shoes and a helmet two sizes too big, and everybody laughed at me," he says. "I was riding with guys who were older than me. I thought, 'They're too good. I want to be good like them. I can't get discouraged.' So I got passionate. You can't be afraid of failure, especially on a skateboard, because the ramps are big."

From the start, Antoine wanted to be good at it. He saw older kids who had sponsors, and he set out to get sponsored too, although he thought he'd have to wait until he was fifteen. But his hard, daily practice paid off sooner than he thought it would. By age nine, Antoine was winning competitions, and by age ten, a skateboarding shop asked to be his sponsor. "He could not believe it," his mother remembers. "His jaw just about dropped onto the floor."

Today Antoine has three sponsors. A skateboard clothing firm gives him pants, shirts, backpacks, and hats. A board maker gives him two new skateboards a month—and he goes through them. And a shop covers other costs for him, such as entry to events. This may seem like a delinquent's sport, but in fact there is big money in it. A number of skateboarders every year turn pro, with sponsors eager to use their talents to market high-priced clothing and equipment.

For Antoine, skateboarding makes sense. A kid in a verdant suburb learns golf. A kid whose house is beside a mountain straps on skis. Antoine lives in the heart of the city. And so he sails on his skateboard, smoothing off the hard edges of the cement world that surrounds him, his small frame dancing a graceful ballet on the sidewalks, stairs, and streets.

More importantly, big cities can be lonely places. Here, among the skateboarders, Antoine belongs. He has friends, and he makes new ones all the time. "At the beginning it was tough to be accepted," he says. "But there were other beginners, and we got better together."

"And it's a lot of fun," says Antoine, "more fun than soccer," which he used to play. "I was tired of kicking a ball. I like to be afraid a bit. I like going fast and high in the air."

He is a small kid, not really big enough for hockey or football. But you don't need to be big to skateboard; in fact, a light, flexible kid such as Antoine is at an advantage. Instead of worrying about being small, he makes the most of what he's got, recovering effortlessly from tumbles that would inflict serious pain on a heavier kid.

On the balcony above the competition, Mathieu Bouffard, the manager, watches as Antoine attempts a midair jump on a ramp, misses it, falls, and springs back onto his board. "The difference between him and me," says Mathieu, who is twenty-three, "is that I wouldn't have been able to get up from that fall."

Despite the fall, Antoine is smokin' today. Of seventeen kids enrolled in the competition, all but two are eliminated. It's now a showdown between Antoine and Scott, a seventeen-year-old who stands fully a head taller than Antoine and has been skateboarding for twice as long.

Scott goes first, tries a trick, and slams into the wall. But he continues, and completes a skillful run. Antoine follows him. He does well at first, then falls twice. It is clear that Antoine has lost. As the manager hands Scott the $100 prize money, Antoine stands to one side, silent.

"You have to persevere and have confidence in yourself," says Antoine afterwards, already spouting the patter of a seasoned athlete. "If you miss a trick you start over and you will eventually get a good result. I was a bit disappointed, but I came in second. I lost but I'm satisfied. I am the equal of a guy who is seventeen years old."

Brody Lampreau, age 10

Ten years ago, in a Native community of the
Shushwap First Nation, nestled in a western
mountain range, a boy named Brody was born.
Brody's biological mother, Roberta, was only
eighteen at the time, and quickly realized she didn't
have the means to take care of a child. So when Brody
was three months old, she named her parents, Marion and Roy,
as her son's legal guardians.

Roberta made the right choice for her son. Marion is a
generous, loving woman, and Roy is a guy you like right away. In
a big booming voice, Roy admits he did some crazy stuff in his
life. But he quit drinking thirteen years ago, and now he's a solid
family man. He's worked in a sawmill for thirty years—two
weeks of day shifts, two weeks of nights. When he gets home,
he takes Bear, the family dog, for a walk, and then carries in a
few armloads of wood to heat the house for the night.

Roy and Marion, who had four daughters of their own and no
sons, took to Brody right away. "He's my little boy,"
Roy says. But as Brody grew, Marion and Roy noticed he was
different than other children his age. At six months, he still wasn't
making any sounds. They took him to a doctor, who sent him to a
specialist. The specialist said Brody suffers from fetal alcohol

syndrome. Due to his condition, Brody lacks muscle tone in his limbs, jaws, and tongue, making it difficult for him to speak.

"A lot of people said when we first started that he wouldn't be able to learn or do math," says Roy. But Roy wasn't discouraged. He fired up his three-quarter-ton pick-up, a battered old 1973 Ford, and he and Marion drove young Brody down to the speech therapist, a one-hour drive each way. At first, all Brody could do was grunt. Determined to help their son, Marion and Roy continued taking Brody to the speech therapist every month, then twice a month, then every week. "It was a really long process," Marion recalls. "But with a lot of help, he started talking. He spoke twenty words at age four."

Then Marion enlisted the help of all the other little kids at Brody's daycare, where she worked. At snack time, each boy or girl had to say what they wanted, "juice" or "apple" or "banana." Brody just pointed. Eventually, he said "uce," as close as he could get to juice. Or she would put a box of cereal on the table with no bowl, spoon, or milk, forcing Brody to use his words. "We did the same thing over and over again and it took a lot of work," Marion says. By age five, Brody could say 300 words.

Today Brody has risen to not only equal the other kids in fifth grade but has actually surpassed many of them in spelling, reading comprehension, and math. It turns out that Brody's brain works just fine—though he has trouble holding a pencil, and needs his parents' help at night to complete his homework. Brody has made the most of two things: his sharp mind and his community's support. The town believed in him, and he hasn't let them down. He even helps the other kids figure out games on the computer.

"He does the best he can do," says Roy. Brody likes to do well and appreciates his father's encouragement. "I do it to get an A," he says. "I got a high mark and Dad was so happy he gave me enough money to buy a Pokémon Silver for Gameboy, a pocket monster game."

It helps a lot that Brody is in a small class. There are only twenty-seven kids in his Neqweyqwelsten School (Neqweyqwelsten is Shushwap for "By the creek"). "We care about the kids individually and try to cater to their exact needs," says Cindy Matthew, Brody's teacher. Cindy also gives her students ten cents credit for every word they get right in a weekly spelling test. So far, Brody's earned enough to buy a backpack and a mirror for his mother. And on a recent quiz, he earned another dollar for spelling the following words correctly: arrived, followed, guessed, seemed, colored, rounded, flipped, grabbed, fried, and tried. "He gets really good at math remembering how much he's earned," Marion laughs.

Sharon Antoniak, an early childhood consultant who has worked with Brody for six years, says it's very rare for a Native child with fetal alcohol syndrome to blossom as Brody has done. Most get bounced from specialist to specialist, and many end up in jail. "He's had support throughout the entire community, and that has really made the difference," she says.

Brody's determination and positive attitude have also been key to his success. And his parents, whom he considers his best friends, have played an instrumental role in building his self-confidence. Every morning before Brody wakes up, Roy scribbles a note and leaves it on the fridge: "Have a good day, Son. Love, Dad." And every evening when he gets home, he asks, "How much homework do you have to do?" On weekends in warm weather, Roy takes Brody fishing for trout in the creek.

Roy and Marion know that in high school Brody won't get the individual care he now has, and that worries them. "I'm afraid that if he can't keep up, they'll just push him aside," Roy says. But for now, he's content to be proud of his son. "One parent up here said he wouldn't amount to anything," he says. "Now Brody's made him eat his own words."

4 Stick with It and Try Your Hardest

Zoë Pollard, age 7

Zoë Pollard's mother, Beth, had always played piano, and dreamed that one day her daughter would do the same. But they didn't have a piano. Then one morning in May, Zoë and Beth stopped at a little Cape Cod-style house in their neighborhood. An elderly couple who had lived there many years were moving out, and selling their things at a tag sale. Beth spotted an old upright brown wood piano and bought it for $200.

Now as you know, a piano is not much good if nobody plays it. But, for a year after the movers brought it into Zoë's house, on the outskirts of a big eastern city, the old piano sat there in the living room, out of tune, forlorn and silent. Zoë wanted to learn to play, but Beth couldn't find her a teacher. "We interviewed a stuffy lady, but we didn't connect," says Beth. Then they found Shari Weisz. "She was lovely," says Beth.

But Miss Shari (as Zoë calls her teacher) wasn't sure she wanted Zoë as a student. "I was going over the policy letter, and when I mentioned workshops and recitals, she started to cry," the teacher recalls. "If you can't get a student to play at a level where they're solid enough to perform, what's the point? I was on the fence. Did I want to take somebody on who didn't want to perform?"

She decided to try, and Zoë started piano lessons in August.

At first all went well. The sheets of beginner music all had little cartoons of puppies and butterflies and flowers on them. Arriving home after school, Zoë would run to the old piano and practice simple songs, to learn fingering and placement.

Then in September, the piano teacher told Zoë that there would be a recital on Halloween, and gave Zoë a sheet of music by Pozzoli that she wanted her to learn, in order to perform a duet with her, the teacher.

"This looked like a real piece of music," says Beth. "Seven grand staffs with both hands playing together. Zoë just broke down and sobbed right there."

Zoë was terrified. Beth decided to try to help her. She scanned the sheet of music into her computer, and then separated the piece into different parts, and made the notes bigger and easier to see.

As Beth remembers, "Zoë witnessed me scanning it, breaking it down. I said, 'You don't have to learn the whole thing at once.'"

That helped Zoë a lot. "She just sat down and she was learning it pretty fast."

To Miss Shari, the stage fright was actually a sign of talent in Zoë. "Talented kids tend to be a little more sensitive, a little more temperamental," she says. Still, Zoë's parents were worried, so they took her to see a child therapist, Sherry Minniti D'Elia, to see what was causing her performance anxiety.

"It was a fear of making a mistake. She was afraid people would be mad at her and not like her if she made a mistake," the therapist explains. "She felt responsible somehow for making people happy." For several weeks, Sherry the therapist worked with Zoë, to help her learn to believe in herself and not feel it was her job to make other people happy.

Zoë's parents' support, her own practicing, and the therapy all helped. On the day of the recital (which Beth renamed a 'piano party' to make it sound like more fun), fifteen students gathered in the teacher's house. "Zoë ran to the piano when Robert finished," as Beth describes it. "She did two duets with the teacher and one piece all by herself." Zoë felt tremendously proud. "I played 'On Two Wheels' and 'When Daylight Ends,'" Zoë recalls.

Zoë's battle with stage fright was not over, though. One evening a few weeks later, Beth went to pick her up at Brownies. Her troop was making plans for an upcoming Christmas talent show for Edge Hill, a local seniors' residence.

"All the other girls are up and dancing and talking about what they are going to do, and she is literally in a ball in the corner," Beth recalls. Zoë was crying, and too scared to take part.

Beth had an idea. "It occurred to me that this home probably had a piano," she says. "I asked if Zoë could play some music." Zoë agreed. She worked on some music pieces to perform. "I practice every morning and every night," says Zoë. "Like when I have free time after school or after dinner."

With all that practice, the Christmas concert turned out to be fun!

Zoë had now done two successful shows. She was beginning to feel pretty confident about going out there to play piano in public. In fact, she felt so good that she was ready to do something incredible: give support to someone who also had stage fright. That someone, believe it or not, was her father, Dave.

Her piano teacher, Miss Shari, was planning a Christmas recital. Dave, Zoë's father, announced that he wanted to play a piano duet of "Silent Night" with Zoë. "He jumped right up and said he was going to do this," says Beth. "I don't think he realized how much work it takes to do something like this."

This time, Zoë wasn't the problem: it was her dad. "She was very confident," says Miss Shari. "But when they tried playing together, it was a disaster. He kept stopping. I emailed Beth and I said, 'If he doesn't feel he's able to do it, I'll just play the duet with her.' "

For Zoë, this proved a nice boost – to realize that, at least in playing the piano, she was more confident than her father.

"I was a lot more nervous than she was," admits Dave. "In some ways it was a really great thing to do – to illustrate the point that it's okay to be nervous, and you can take chances."

In the end, Zoë helped her father to make it through the song. "She's a very solid performer," says her teacher. "There were no hitches. She was keeping eye contact with Dave. She had to slow down her tempo so he could keep up. In the end, he played one arpeggio per measure and it was fine."

Thanks to a lot of practice, and with the support of her teacher and her parents, Zoë today is comfortable playing piano in public. Now whether she continues to play music or moves on to other pursuits, she will always know one thing: that she can overcome fear through hard work and believing in herself.

Adrian Morningstar, age 9

Adrian Morningstar missed thirty-five days of school last year. This year, he has missed twenty-five. Adrian is not playing hooky. Far from it: he keeps on getting parts in big professional musicals and operas as an actor, singer, and dancer.

Adrian has performance in his blood. His mom and dad first met at age seven and eight, when they shared the stage in a production of *Finnian's Rainbow*, the classic Broadway musical. A photograph of his parents from that show, both wearing way too much makeup, now occupies a treasured place on the piano. So it was no surprise when Michael, Adrian's father, cut out an ad in the newspaper two years ago that said: "Kids Wanted!"

The ad was for the musical *Oliver*, and specified the following: "Boys aged seven to fifteen with unbroken voices. Girls aged ten to twelve and waif-like in appearance. All children will sing 'Consider Yourself' and must be five feet and under in height."

Although Adrian's older sister sang in a choir, she was too tall to meet the ad's requirements. But Adrian, who had never sung or danced on stage, decided to give it a shot. He rehearsed for a few days, and then headed over to the rehearsal hall with his father. "Wow! There are tons and tons of people here,"

Adrian recalls thinking. He rode an elevator to the rehearsal room, where, in front of twenty other kids, he sang the song he had learned.

"There was this one lady who said, 'You can go down the elevator,' or 'You can stay with me,' " he remembers. Adrian got to stay, and the lady invited him to a second audition the next morning. Adrian recalls the second audition clearly: after more singing, the kids were told to sit in a line and do nothing for fifteen minutes while the judges watched. Those who fidgeted or talked got cut. Adrian now understands that to succeed as an actor you have to prove that you can follow instructions.

Arriving home for lunch, he told his mom, Joanne: "I have to dance this afternoon!" While Adrian was calm, his parents admit they were petrified. "Adrian had never danced," says his mother. "I thought, 'Oh my God! What are they going to ask him to do?' I asked him, 'Adrian, can you do this?' " She gets up and marches along the floor: Stomp! clap! stomp! clap! Adrian could do that, and much more. That night, he came home beaming. He'd learned a whole routine!

On the weekend, Adrian went to still more auditions, trying out for the role of Oliver himself. He didn't get that role, and waited a month to know whether he had a part at all. Finally, the call came, and it was immortalized in a note that his mom left for his sister. Now pasted in Adrian's scrapbook, the note says: "Adrian got in—Fagin's gang! One of twenty kids out of 500 to 600."

As Adrian soon realized, the real challenges had just begun.

It's not always easy being a child performer. You're up late, you can't watch your favorite TV shows, and you have to work doubly hard to stay caught up with homework. His rehearsals ran from two in the afternoon to eight thirty at night all through October, so he left school early every day, and snatched moments during rehearsal breaks to do homework.

One evening, he was rushing more than usual to finish his homework. The assignment consisted of reading a five-page story and answering questions. Hurried to get it over with, he accidentally grabbed his notebook and opened it upside down, filling a few pages with his answers. When his mom went to get him after school the next day, he was crying. "I hate my teacher," he told his mom. "She wants me to do all my homework over because I did it upside down." Luckily, after Joanne had a few words with the principal, the teacher relented.

Oliver itself went off without a hitch for eighty-six performances. Unfortunately, the adult cast neglected to invite the child actors to the closing night party. (This oversight reminded some of the play itself, in which children are abandoned to an orphanage and forced to beg for food.) But the kids didn't let this exclusion get them down. The child actors and their parents organized their own party at a pub near the theatre. "We had fun," says Adrian. "We played pool and shuffleboard."

All in all, Adrian had a great time. He was ready for more, and soon after landed the part of Michael in a Christmas pantomime production of *Peter Pan*. Later, he was cast as a midshipman in *Billy Budd*, an opera set in 1797 on the

British naval vessel *Indomitable*. It's a tricky part: in front of an audience of thousands, Adrian must step nimbly among about sixty cast members who continuously clamber on and off a hydraulic platform that never stops rising, tilting, and spinning to suggest a ship at sea. And, as was common on such ships, he has the honor of being flogged with a whip during the performance (he wears protection under his shirt).

So between theatre, grade five, and homework, Adrian is a busy kid. On top of that, there are tryouts for parts in television commercials and shows, and movies. There, Adrian has been less fortunate: he has been to fifteen auditions, and not once been chosen. "The good thing is that no one calls you and says, 'You don't have it, you're just too bad,' " Adrian reasons. "The dark side is nobody calls and says 'You do have it.' "

Despite numerous rejections, Adrian doesn't give up. He continues to audition for parts, always remaining optimistic. "I know there are going to be more opportunities," he says. "There are so many shows, so you know there are chances of you getting a part. You go into Greek City Videos down the street and you see there's like 1,000 videos."

"Besides," he says, "going to auditions is fun."

David Armstrong, age 11

It's Saturday afternoon at the Milk International Children's Festival of the Arts. The hosting city's lakeshore is festooned with flags and tents, and droves of children bustle from one performance to the next. David Armstrong is on stage in the Children's Own Museum space, performing a magic show. Sitting cross-legged on the floor are thirty little kids, their eyes wide open.

"This is my wallet," David says, unfolding a large black wallet made of stiff cardboard. "Since it is a magician's wallet," he jokes, "it is of course empty. But anyway," he continues, "who needs money to buy flowers for their girlfriend, when they can just grow flowers directly in their wallet?"

David turns the wallet over and opens it. At this point, colored paper flowers are supposed to pop out. Only they don't. David turns the wallet and unfolds it again. No flowers.

David starts to panic. The kids are staring. He has to do something, so he thinks fast. "Well, that wallet just doesn't want to perform magic for you today," he tells the crowd. "But maybe this pack of cards will." And, as smoothly as he can, he moves into a card trick.

David tells me this story a few months later, when I visit him at his house. "If you get it wrong and you're on stage, just go with it and make a joke out of it," he explains. He says it's the spectators that drive him to go on, even when the show is in trouble. "When I see the audience go 'Wow,' it's strengthening for me, and that's what has given me the motivation to go this far."

The day I meet David, I ring the doorbell and he answers, barefoot, wearing an untucked dress shirt over track pants. He holds out his hand and shakes mine firmly. "How's your day so far?" he asks, looking me in the eye.

His mom comes downstairs and they lead me into the living room. On the coffee table, David has set up a magician's tools: tubes filled with colored balls, packs of cards, handkerchiefs, and magic wands. "Well, David's got it all set up here," his mother, Johanna, says, surprised. "I've been busy upstairs, I didn't even know what he was doing down here." Self-sufficient, David doesn't need any help preparing for a show.

He starts with the simplest of tricks: He takes a penny in his right hand, drops it into his left, then holds out his left hand to hand me the penny. Oops! His left hand is empty; with his right hand he plucks the penny from my ear. Easy? Go ahead and try it!

"I've been practicing that trick for three years," David says. "Over and over and over again, every day." David first got the magic bug at age six, when his mom enrolled him in an afterschool class run by a magician named Magic Mike.

"The first class I took with Mike started with the spiked coin trick," David wrote in a newspaper article about himself, published in the *National Post*. "When Mike showed it to us we all thought it would be harder than writing 3,000 math tests, but it was really very easy."

David was hooked. Unlike other kids who lose interest after learning two or three tricks, he stuck with it. He began reading every magic catalogue he could find. Friends and family gave him catalogues from magic shops in Hollywood, London, and Toronto. Two school friends, Matthew and Max, started doing tricks with him. Every day during recess he practiced in front of other kids in the schoolyard. His parents bought him more tricks. "At Christmas, I don't get anything else other than tricks," he says.

Best of all, his parents dug into the back of a cupboard and found a black beaver fur top-hat that had belonged to David's great-grandfather. "They had a hat that was a symbol of a magician!" David says, his eyes sparkling. "I usually have a girl come up on stage and hold the hat."

According to David, it takes more than cool hats and expensive tricks to make a good magician, though. "David Ben was famous not because of his tricks," he says. "I could buy them for twenty-four dollars each. He got famous because of his patter. The trick instructions never come with a good patter."

"You can't just say, 'Here's a ball.' You have to say, 'Here's a ball, his name is Eddy, he went to school and his math test was wrong. The teacher took out a feather and chopped off his head and then he was gone.'"

One of David's teachers noticed his passion for magic and called the Children's Own Museum. They invited him to be the first child ever to perform on their stage.

"It was amazing," says Gerry Mabin, who booked the show. "The children down there just loved it. A teacher said on her way out, 'The highlight was David Armstrong.' He's performed several times now. It's good for him, and good for the other children to see that if you really work at something, you can really achieve."

Magic helps David to feel good about himself. The first time he saw a show, he noticed that the spectators were completely in awe of the magician. "Look at the audience," he thought. "This is cool." Now, he has learned to work a crowd in the same way. "I really try to involve the audience," he says. "I try to get them laughing, motivated—we all have fun together."

The children's museum pays David for each show with a twenty-five dollar coupon to a magic store in town. This helps to keep his act fresh and lets David know that his work is appreciated. As a result, he's always eager to go back and perform again. "I know all the people at the museum. They're all excited when I come. I thought my show would be a one-time thing, but now I've done seven of them."

Magic Mike Segal, David's first teacher, is living proof of what can be achieved through the power of magic. Mike started performing when he was eleven, too. Now, at age thirty-five, he has his own daily television show, runs magic camps in both the U.S. and Canada, and has performed around the world.

Mike says many kids find magic empowering because it's the first time they get to fool their parents without lying. They say, "Wow, I can do something that they cannot." Plus, he says, magic teaches kids to solve problems and overcome shyness in public. "I know it helped me overcome my fear of public speaking and performing in front of a crowd."

Update

David Armstrong, *now* age 15

Five years later, David Armstrong has changed a lot. At age 11 he was a slightly pudgy boy, passionate about magic, brimming with self-confidence. Today, at 15, he's tall and lanky, in tip-top shape. He's in his third year at an elite all-boys private school, where he has joined the rowing team. That means he has to get up at 5:30 a.m. for training, in winter. In summer, he has to be on the lake at 5:30 a.m. His hands are split from the oars. And he has figured out that life is a lot more complex than he thought it was when he was 11. He has to start planning for his future, and he finds that challenging.

Even so, David is up to his old tricks. "I'm still doing magic," he says. "Now I practice more on my own. I muck around more with cards. I'm spending less money on it and going back to the basics." When he's studying he takes a break and picks up a deck, to practice a trick. I ask him to show me something. He disappears upstairs, returns with a deck of cards, and launches into a story about the difference between gamblers and magicians. One by one, he pulls the kings from the deck, showing me each king before putting it face down on the coffee table. Then he turns them over: magically, they have become 4s. He then pulls the kings from the middle of the deck.

"Looking back on the secret" he says, "it's still completely true with me. If you're going to do something, don't do it half-heartedly." That's how he approaches rowing. "It hurts. It's hard because I wasn't very athletic at the time. I was slightly overweight. Now I'm under 159 pounds – I'm mid weight." He likes rowing, he says, because everyone supports each other: "It's good to know that although you're hurting, you're not alone."

Along with rowing, David has landed a part in the school's production of *King Lear*. David chose rowing and acting over magic he says, because his school encourages those activities. It was a difficult decision, though.

"As much as I like those activities, I'm not as passionate for them as I am for magic," says David, whose father owns a multi-national company. "In our society, being a professional magician isn't going to work. I was a little bit mad when I realized that that's the way the world works – that magic isn't really a career that can pay as well."

Still, last summer David went to magic camp again. He vows to never give it up. After all, he points out, his idol David Ben ditched a career in tax law to become a highly successful magician, and has since written a book on how magic can help you in business.

"Whatever career I choose," David says, "magic is always going to be there."

Sophie Hsu, age 11

There are some children whose talents just make your jaw drop to the floor. Sophie Hsu is one of them. In her living room, she sits down at her Kawai piano, her feet in her Hello Kitty slippers barely reaching the pedals. "This is a new piece by Chopin that I don't know too well," she says. "So I may make some mistakes."

And then she begins to play, with no music in front of her, her fingers poised upright on the keyboard like ballet dancers standing on tiptoe, prancing and pouncing on the keys, quickly and confidently. If she made any mistakes, I sure couldn't tell. Wow.

Sophie Hsu began playing piano at age four. She loved it. Within three months, she gave her first concert at a seniors' home in her neighborhood. She has never looked back. In her house, on the mantlepiece, beside the silk tapestry of Buddha and a glass bristling with sticks of incense, sits a trophy crowned with a golden grand piano—the highest music award for children in Sophie's region. She is the only child to have won the trophy two years in a row.

Sophie's repertoire includes Bach, Beethoven, Haydn, and Mozart. Since the age of five, she has been continuously winning first place in her age group at classical music festivals.

"Music is beautiful," Sophie says. "And I love applause. I like it when people enjoy my music."

Sophie's parents immigrated from Taiwan thirteen years ago, seeking a better education for their kids. It has not been easy—the family knew no one. More recently, Sophie's father has moved back to Taiwan to look after his ailing mother.

Sophie now lives with her mother and two elder siblings in a comfortable, yet not particularly rich, neighborhood. Every morning Sophie catches the bus near her house and then transfers to the subway to go to her public school in the heart of downtown.

The school is straight out of that movie *Fame*, about New York kids at a performing arts academy that has no money for repairs but where creativity seems to seep from cracks in the floor. The 100-year-old building serves 1,300 students from kindergarten through high school. Its dirty linoleum floors are a patchwork of colors, the lockers are dented, and the walls scream for a coat of paint.

Yet murals in crazy colors cheer things up. And if you peer through classroom door windows, you'll be treated to inspiring scenes: rooms full of teens, sitting on mismatched chairs, diligently practicing the violin. The students here focus on choir, theatre, painting, sculpture, and wind, string, and percussion instruments. Sophie, who has always attended this school, plays the flute, and has also accompanied the school orchestra on piano.

Sophie had a tough time when she entered school: she

knew no one and could speak only Mandarin. But she found that through music she could express what she could not put into words. "Sometimes languages are difficult for me, so, through my actions, I can show people that I love them very much," she says. She has a deep, innocent passion for music that she just wants to share. "Music is beautiful and I love it very, very, very, very much," she says, her eyes sparkling like black pearls. "And I really like it when people smile."

For seven years, Sophie has stuck with Wei-Sze Chang, her piano teacher. Ms. Chang trained and taught for many years in Austria before moving to North America in 1980. She says that from the first time she met Sophie, who was then four, she knew she had a gifted pupil.

"When she came to me I already felt the piano was not a

stranger to her," says Ms. Chang. "Right away her fingers were standing up on the keys. Usually it takes me three months to get students to hold their hands in the right position. And she has perfect pitch. I said 'do re me,' and she could find them right away on the keyboard."

The teacher sets a demanding schedule: Sophie has a three-hour lesson every Friday night, and then plays all weekend. Ms. Chang calls between eight and ten times every weekend to ask Sophie how her work is progressing. "I work hard," Sophie says. "I don't give up what I love and what I want."

Sophie's willpower is the key to her success, her teacher says. "Some people are very talented but too sensitive. To be good you have to be very strong. I remember one time we were in Toronto. Sophie was tired, her sister was tired, and it was nine o'clock at night. We had already practiced for nine hours. I was so tired I said we should stop. But Sophie said, 'The piece is so beautiful. I'm just getting started.'"

Sophie knows how to conserve her energy for when she needs it. Ms. Chang recalls the time when Sophie had just returned from a trip to Taiwan: "It is a long flight, and Sophie arrived at her lesson, asleep in her father's arms. He lay her down on the sofa and she slept until it was time for her lesson. Then she woke up, played beautifully, and lay down and went back to sleep. I said 'This girl is really going to be something.'"

Piano recitals are not always easy for Sophie. Travel and the stress of competing can be tough. Two years ago she went to a music competition on the other side of the continent. The air travel made her sick, and when she arrived she couldn't eat, and she was exhausted and feverish. Still, she put on her lucky red bead necklace, persevered, performed, and took second prize.

Although Sophie didn't place first that time, she took it all in stride. "For me it's not winning that matters, it's doing my best," she says. She sees competitions as opportunities to learn and improve. "When I was a kid I didn't understand anything the judges were saying so I waited for the judges' scores," she says. "But now I don't wait for the scores, I wait for the judges' commentary."

Sophie also waits for the applause. "When she is loved, it is encouragement," says her elder sister, Emilie, a twenty-one-year-old law student. "It is a source of energy for her."

5 Don't Be Afraid to Try New Things

Sam Friedman, age 12

Last summer Sam Friedman and his family moved from a town in the Rust Belt to a community on the Eastern Seaboard. Sam didn't waste any time signing up for a new activity. On his first day in the new town, he attended his first-ever Boy Scouts' meeting. Although he's now glad he took that first step, he admits that it was pretty scary at the time.

"I was surrounded by all these kids who knew all the knots and badges," he recalls. "It was just a little embarrassing." Then the Scout leader told him the troop was leaving for camp that Sunday for two weeks—and it was already Wednesday! "Would you like to join us?" the leader asked.

"Sure," said Sam. "The idea of Scouts excited me and I just wanted to try it," he explained later. "I figured it would be fun. Unless I know there's a real problem with something, I usually try it before I make a decision."

The Scout leader had only one condition. To attend camp, Sam would have to memorize the Scout Oath, Law, Motto, and Slogan. With only four days to meet his goal, Sam went straight to work. Practicing every day, he memorized everything on time. "Then I went to the leader's house, and I said, 'I want to go on the trip.' And he said, 'All right, let's hear what you know.'"

"On my honor I will do my best to do my duty to God and my country; to obey the Scout Oath; to help other people at all times; to keep myself physically strong, mentally awake, and morally straight," answered Sam, quoting the Scout's Oath. He successfully repeated the rest of what he'd learned, earning his place among the campers.

Sam had almost no time to prepare for the trip. He didn't know anyone, and he'd never been to sleepover camp. Plus, he has Tourette's Syndrome, a brain condition which causes him to fidget and make facial expressions he cannot control. He didn't know how the Scouts would react, so he was pretty nervous about leaving his family. Still, he says, "I figured it would be more fun than if I stayed at home."

"One of the kids had a big mouth and he told everybody I have Tourette's," he recalls. "I did not need everybody to know that. It did bug me, but fortunately everybody forgot about it after the first day."

In the end, Sam had fun at camp, and did well. He earned four merit badges: swimming, metalwork, arts, and leatherwork. Having never swum more than twenty-five yards at once, at camp he swam 150 yards. He also helped cook, learned CPR, and endured mosquitoes. And with the boys in his tent staying up late into the night, he learned to operate on very little sleep. "I had to survive it, I guess," Sam says.

Sam gets his adventurous streak from his parents. As a young man, Sam's father, Doug, moved to Mexico City, a place he did not know, to work on a newspaper. There he met and fell in love with a Mexican woman named Fidelia, whom he later married. Then, Fidelia gathered enough courage to leave her own country to join Doug in his.

Sam, the eldest of three children, has always been a high achiever. He has done well at school, soccer, and tae kwon do. He also speaks fluent Hebrew. From a very early age, he wrote little illustrated books with titles like "Mean People," "Planets," and "My Dream." Then, in second grade, he decided to try something more challenging: he began writing "The Secret Key," a seventy-page chapter book.

"I remember we were discussing the fact that Isaac Asimov had written 400 books," his father recalls. "So I guess Sam figured he'd better get started if he wanted to catch him." Plus Sam got hooked on the *Goosebumps* books by R. L. Stein. "I must have mentioned that Stein made a lot of money," Sam's father adds.

Sam needed no further incentive. He started writing most days after school. "I looked at my notes and thought, 'What if I made my main character, Jack, do this?'" The mystery novel tells of the adventures of three boys — Jack, Jordan, and Jake — who go shopping at a mall and find an enchanted key. An evil sorcerer emerges from the key, and sends them back in time. Sam first wrote the book longhand, then typed it on a computer. Now, he and his father are searching for a publisher.

But Sam says the toughest challenge of his life, by far, has been starting grade six at a new school last September. "Welcome to the ultimate scare," he says. "School."

Of all the students there, Sam knew only three. Thanks to

Scouts, he'd already met Harris, Manuel, and Barudh. If Sam hadn't had the courage to join Scouts a few months earlier, starting school would have been that much harder. Seeing a few familiar faces made things a little less harsh.

Even so, the first months were difficult. "Normally," says Sam, "You hear, 'You'll make friends.' At this school it took a full month before someone came over and said, 'Do you want to hang out with me?' Not a lot of people move here, so they don't practice for what happens when a new kid arrives."

While the children at Sam's old school were used to his Tourette's, the kids at his new school were less understanding. The bullies have teased him, calling him 'Sam Fibian.' Sam has responded to this problem with a two-pronged strategy. First, he got the teachers on his side. As well as earning good marks, he behaved well. "I didn't goof around in class. They don't really care about grades, they care more about attitude," he says. Second, he has stood up to the teasing as best he can. "I had to say to the bullies, 'I'm not going to take it,' and not shake," he says.

School, "is one problem that I'm not even half done with," Sam says. But Sam is good at meeting challenges. If he was brave enough to take on Scouts, and the daunting task of writing an entire book in second grade, he will find ways to overcome his problems at school. Already, he has beaten his fear. All that's left for him to do now is to earn the respect he deserves. "If you ever have trouble with other people," Sam advises, "Stand up, show courage, and don't let others get the best of you. Give it what you've got and don't back down."

Update

Sam Friedman, *now* age 16

Sometimes getting fired from a job is the best thing that can happen to you. Here's how it works: You're not happy. Your boss knows it. They fire you. You move on to bigger and better things.

The year he turned sixteen, Sam Friedman landed a summer job at Dairy Queen. He didn't do very well. "I wasn't good at making parfaits," Sam explains. "You take nuts and you take caramel fudge and you have to layer it. I wasn't so good at the layering." He also had problems making novelty Blizzards – specifically, the key lime and banana cream flavors. "I would have customers complain that I didn't put enough bananas in them. I put in more bananas and they said it was too much." Two weeks later: fired. So Sam found a new job, at Rita's Italian Ice. After a month: fired again. Sam just shakes his head. In fast food work, he says, "You have to do whatever the employer wants without asking any questions whatsoever."

Working at restaurants was just not Sam's thing. Today, he is much better off. He works as a soccer referee. Rather than making Blizzards for five dollars and fifty cents an hour, he's in a place where he feels confident: on a soccer field, earning a sweet twenty-two dollars an hour.

On the soccer field, he is learning life lessons too, he says.

Sometimes parents question his rulings. "I've realized that a lot of people are going to criticize you and make you doubt yourself. You have to learn to accept the criticism and move on."

Sam is smart, and brave. In every area of his life, he'd rather try something new than stick around where he's not wanted. Remember those kids who drove him crazy at private school in grade six? Sam had a solution: he transferred to public school.

"The group I was hanging out with wasn't very nice," he says. So he switched schools. He notes, "My dad could then save the money." Clearly, his parents, Doug and Fidelia, raised him right, and they even won recognition for it. In 2005, the American Family Coalition named the couple Parents of the Year in their state.

Now Sam attends a big public high school, with 2,000 students. He doesn't love it. "The school, like many others, is incompetent," he says. Still, he does not dwell on that. Instead, he has taken up new challenges.

When he's not coaching soccer or maintaining a B+ average, Sam is at Scouts. He is now a Life Scout, and needs just three badges to rise to the top rank: Eagle.

In high school, he has enrolled in two demanding sports: track and cross-country running.

"I run three miles, in the woods and up hills," he says. "It's hard work, but I'll keep doing it. Hopefully next year I'll be even better."

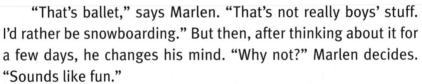

Marlen Zuyderhoff-Gray, age 11

It's a snowy evening in December. Marlen Zuyderhoff-Gray is sitting at the kitchen table doing his homework when Flinder, his older sister, arrives from a dance class. "Guess what?" she says. "The performing arts center is looking for boys to dance in its holiday performance of *The Nutcracker*."

"That's ballet," says Marlen. "That's not really boys' stuff. I'd rather be snowboarding." But then, after thinking about it for a few days, he changes his mind. "Why not?" Marlen decides. "Sounds like fun."

The next Saturday afternoon, Marlen is thrown into a completely new world. The arts center is full of girls, costumes, and mysterious long corridors leading to changing rooms. A vast stage is lit with thousands of lights.

In the show, Marlen plays the part of a little boy unwrapping his gifts on Christmas morning. That part's okay, but the costume is not: Marlen's wearing tights and really short shorts with suspenders—English schoolboy stuff.

"I'm like, 'Why am I in these?' It's the complete opposite of what I wear. I thought everyone would look at me like an idiot." But no one did, and in the end, Marlen loved acting in *The Nutcracker*. "Sometimes you've gotta try something different, so

I tried it and I had a great time," he admits later.

Marlen likes to try new things. Whether it's break-dancing or making new friends or creating a giant dragon for a party, he's ready to give it a shot. And he is rarely disappointed.

His creative, adventurous streak has a lot to do with the way he was raised. He grew up on a farm, as part of a community who left the city behind in the 1970s to make a go of it on the land. They settled in a verdant area of rolling hills, rich farmland, pine forests, and crystal-clear lakes. In the summer they built tree forts, and in the winter they built snow forts.

Rather than send their children to school, Marlen's parents decided to teach them at home. His mom taught the three Rs while his father gave music lessons. By the time Marlen first set foot in a classroom, he was in grade three.

Those years outside the school system didn't hurt him. In fact today he's a good student, plus he has a bold and imaginative mind. Marlen loves to play sports, too, a passion he got from his father, Cameron. He especially enjoys soccer, and his team even won the tournament last season. But winning, says Marlen, is not the only point of playing.

"You can't always win, I mean, come on," he says. "It's not fun for the other players. There're some total ball hogs. I'm the complete opposite. I want other people to cooperate. I try to make sure that everyone has fun. You don't want them to be sad that they didn't do anything. I get a few goals. I mostly pass to other people. I want other people who haven't scored to have a chance."

The youngest of three children, Marlen learned how to be generous from his brother and sister. While many elder siblings would tell their little brother to get lost, according to Marlen, Orion and Flinder are understanding and encouraging. His brother, for example, helped him learn to snowboard, showing him the technique for carving his way down a hill.

Like everyone, Marlen sometimes struggles to stay disciplined. For a time, he was seduced by television. "We had cable for a month," says Marlen. "I would go home and I didn't even care about my homework. I would just be watching TV. There is some good stuff like *Star Trek*, but all those other shows are just complete utter junk, and they take a hole out of your life. We cancelled the cable."

Marlen faces other challenges, too. It isn't always easy being different. On the farm where he grew up he became fast friends with two girls. "They were the best, they were the bomb," he says. "They totally understood me and I totally understood them." But when he moved to town, he found it tough to adjust to the schoolyard, where boys hang out with boys and girls hang out with girls. "Most guys are like, 'Girls, yuck.' But I'm not like that," he explains. So Marlen innocently tried to make friends with the girls at school, but his attempts backfired. The girls weren't used to hanging out with boys, and reacted badly to Marlen's efforts. "Sometimes the girls were really mean and awful," he says. "But they got over it."

At other times, not being afraid of girls has worked to Marlen's advantage. He got along fine with the girls in the cast of *The Nutcracker*. "At *The Nutcracker* there were, like, lots of girls," he says. "They would invite me over to their locker room."

When it comes to coping with peer pressure, having a supportive mother really helps. Marlen doesn't feel the need to behave just like every other boy, which leaves him open to trying new things. Olga encourages her children, and doesn't expect Marlen to always be tough and macho. "Some kids, when they're sick, their parents will say, 'You have to go to school,' " explains Marlen. "My mom will wrap me in a blanket. And if I'm having trouble with anything, I can tell her. She doesn't yell."

All kids face scary challenges: learning to ride a bike, moving to a new school, trying out for the volleyball team. Marlen's strategy is to start with something manageable, and once he's mastered that, he tries something more difficult—all the while making sure to be safe.

"I was looking to overcome my fears at the cottage," Marlen recalls. Watching others carefully and asking for pointers, he psyched himself up for a new challenge. "I jumped off a twelve-foot cliff into the water. Then I went to sixteen feet. It's scary at first and then it'll be fine. It's like being afraid of the dark. You can't be afraid if you know what's there. You jump and you have a few seconds to think, 'What did I do that for?' and, 'Well, I guess I can't go back now,' and then you hit."

Deborah Conway, age 11

Boys play hockey—they've been doing that forever. Girls play hockey too these days, mostly with other girls. Then there's Deborah Conway: she's been playing hockey for eight years. But when Deborah plays, she's usually the only girl on the ice.

I first meet Deborah on a Friday, the last evening of a week-long hockey skills camp. She walks into the dressing room and puts down a black hockey bag that's as big as she is. Then she leaves to use the washroom before suiting up, and I'm left with eight boys, all ten- and eleven-year-olds, lacing up skates and pulling on jerseys.

I tell them I'm here to write a story about Deborah, the only girl among thirty kids at this camp. "We've got another girl here," one guy says, pointing to a boy who's snapping on his helmet. Another boy walks in. "Oh, here's another girl," says the smart aleck. "Now we have three girls."

Ah yes. The changing room. That temple of manliness. It would seem this is no place for a girl—especially a sweet-looking girl like Deborah who's half the size of some of the boys here. But that's where the boys are wrong. Deborah is here because she is a very good hockey player. And if that bothers some boys, well, that's their problem.

Deborah comes in and suits up: Jill strap. Garter belt. Shin pads. Socks. Tape to hold socks on shin pads. Suspenders. Pants. Skates (Dad laces them up). Elastic band for pony tail. Elbow pads. Shoulder and chest pads. Wrist guards. Jersey. Mouth guard. Helmet. She has a blank, determined, faraway look in her eyes, a kind of marble warrior face. Finally, she pulls down her face mask and slips on her gloves.

On the rink the instructor is running through a drill. "Delay, adjust, react!" he yells. This is Deborah's favorite place on earth. At age four, she made it clear she had zero interest in figure skates. "Can I get hockey skates?" she asked. "Can I get black skates?"

From age three, she played ball hockey on the street. In the basement she has whacked thousands of pucks against a wall, trying to hit a suspended box. The wall is covered in black marks. "We could never paint that, could we?" says her mom, brimming with pride.

Early on, Deborah expressed an interest in TV hockey stars: "When I was watching the NHL I'd always be like, 'Where are the girls?' " Then her father took her to the Women's World Hockey Championship. "It was cool, watching all these women playing hockey and then knowing, yeah, I could do it, because it wasn't just for boys," she recalls.

Back in Deborah's neighborhood, there was no girls' league. At age six, she signed up anyway, opting to play on a "mixed" team. At the time, there was only about one girl per club. Since then most girls have switched to girls' leagues or dropped out.

Through practice, Deborah improved. Tiny, gritty, and determined, by age ten she'd earned a slot on a AA team, the second-highest ranking in the sport. Wearing the number nine, she plays forward on the AA team, where she's one of just two girls in the thirteen teams at this level. On her school hockey team, Deborah is the only girl.

Boys who see her for the first time have their doubts about her, she says. "I remember my first game last season. I knew only two people on the team; I think the others kind of assumed, 'Oh, she's a girl, she's probably not very good.' We were losing 1–0 with less than one minute left. So I get this pass and I was on a breakaway; I deke out the goalie and I score. Then it was kind of like I'd broken the wall between me and them so now they could trust me."

But it's not all glory. Deborah takes just as many, if not more, body checks as the guys on her team. "If I'd be going for the puck someone would check me from behind, because I'm the girl," she says. "They'd be like, 'Oh, yeah, I checked the girl.' About six times people were thrown out of the game for checking me from behind. It's not the greatest feeling. But it doesn't stop me from playing hockey because I love it too much to quit."

Despite getting picked on, Deborah keeps her sense of team spirit. According to her mom, after games she says things like "I'm glad we won" or "I'm sorry we lost," not "I was targeted."

The teasing is harder to handle, though. "I was minor novice select and I was skating and someone said, 'Oh, did your nail chip?' " Deborah recalls. Tears well up in her eyes as she tells this story, sitting at her kitchen table, flanked by her parents. "It's not the check that hurts, it's the comments," she says. "The guys are like 'Oh, sissy, oh, sissy,' and that."

It's easier among girls. That much is clear later that day, when Deborah heads to a girls' soccer playoff game. Her marble warrior face is gone. Yet hockey remains her first love, and her room is a shrine to the sport. On the wall is a flag signed by national girls' team players, plus hockey pennants and a picture with hockey legend Bobby Orr. There is a photo of Deborah at age seven, in full hockey gear, with her front teeth missing—not from an errant puck, but just because her baby teeth fell out.

From the windowsill she picks up one bittersweet momento, a puck mounted on a pedestal. "Here's a tournament we were in. I scored three goals so I got the Mr. Hat Trick award."

Many suggest that Deborah switch to girls' hockey now that she's older, but she has decided to stay in the "boys' " league. Not to prove a point, simply so she can improve as a player. "I like a challenge," she says. "I know a lot of the kids on the team. And the boys' teams get a lot more practice and ice time than the girls' teams do."

"Some of my friends dance, some figure skate, some play soccer, and I play hockey," she says reflectively, green eyes sparkling now. "It doesn't matter what other people think. Just do what your heart tells you to do."

6 Be a Loyal Friend

Meaghan Drummond, age 7
Jessica Kowalson, age 8

When I heard about Meaghan Drummond, the young, award-winning humanitarian, I called her right away. As I soon discovered, she is an extremely shy girl—much too shy, in fact, to talk to a reporter. So I mostly talked to her mother and father, and the parents of her good friend Jessica.

When timid Meaghan started kindergarten, she befriended a girl in her class named Jessica Kowalson. Jessica and her twin sister, Jennifer, were born with cerebral palsy, a condition of the brain that affects muscle function. Jessica's case is more severe, and doctors did not expect her to live. Fortunately, Jessica did live—though just barely. She spent the first eighteen months of her life in a hospital, and, since then, has survived twelve surgeries. Today, Jessica is confined to a wheelchair. But through her determination, and with the unwavering support of her parents, teaching assistant, and loyal friend Meaghan, Jessica has truly thrived.

Grace De Thomasis, Jessica's full-time teaching assistant, says most kids at school ignored Jessica—until Meaghan came along. "The majority of kids five and six years old don't worry about a kid that can't move," Grace says. "They don't have that insight."

But Meaghan spotted Jessica right away. "Meaghan sensed that Jessica needed a friend," says Grace. "She treated Jessica like any other child, and yet knew Jessica needed help and was there for her."

Jessica can't move her arms or legs much and has trouble talking. That didn't phase Meaghan. She sat next to her in class, looked at books with her, and pushed her wheelchair to music and gym. When it was time to color, Meaghan helped Jessica switch crayons. She also helped her cut with her special scissors. At recess, she involved Jessica in circle tag, or got Jessica to hold the rope while Meaghan and the other kids skipped. Meaghan even found ways to involve her friend in class chores. She would set Lucky, the class hamster, on Jessica's lap, and wheel him down the hall to clean his cage.

In class, Meaghan helped Jessica hold her hand in the air when she had a question. And when Jessica got her own computer, Meaghan would help her type in her answers. At lunchtime, Meaghan would help Grace feed Jessica.

Like any other kids their age, sometimes the two girls just like to horse around. In the only words quiet little Meaghan dared speak to me, she described a side of Jessica that few others have taken the time to discover: her sense of humor. "When we were in gym on the mats, Jessica would put her foot on me and push me over," recalls Meaghan. "Jessica was laughing."

Jessica isn't the only one who benefits from the special bond she shares with Meaghan. The friendship has helped Meaghan to partly overcome her shyness. "With her clinging to

Jessica, helping Jessica, Meaghan has come out of her shell," says Meaghan's mother. "She needs to be Jessica's voice."

Jessica's parents, Warren and Helen, adore their two daughters, although they admit it can be stressful when others don't understand their family's special needs. Warren breaks down and sobs as he describes how he and his wife were asked to leave their jobs because they were absent so often, caring for Jessica and Jennifer. But when he talks of the Meaghan-Jessica friendship, he brightens up right away, confirming what Meaghan's mom has told me:

"Jessica is just Miss Personality from the start," he says. "And Meaghan is the shyest person. This friendship really brought out Meaghan's personality. She wouldn't say a word to me for two years, and the other day when I saw her she said 'Hi,' no problem."

In the year 2000, Meaghan became the youngest student ever to win the Growing Minds Young Humanitarian Award, given by the teachers in her region. When the television crews came swarming to interview little Meaghan, Jessica had the chance to return her friend's loyalty.

While Meaghan was scared stiff by all the commotion, Jessica, who has participated in fund-raising telethons all her life, wasn't the least bit intimidated. From her wheelchair, she said to Meaghan, "Hold my hand. You're not used to this." And that way, the two friends got through the interviews together.

In grade two, Meaghan moved to a different class than Jessica, just across the hall. The two still hang out together at recess and lunch, and hook up at other times as well. "The other day Meaghan made a cube out of drinking straws in her class, so she came by to show it to Jessica," Grace says. "And at Halloween, Jessica dressed up as Raggedy Ann with a red wig, and she wanted Meaghan to see her."

According to Grace, Meaghan's attitude has set an example for other kids to respect and include Jessica. Now a kid will push Jessica's wheelchair to include her in a game of dodgeball, or give her one end of the skipping rope to turn. But Meaghan's friendship remains the most genuine.

"Meaghan did what she did because of something inside her," says Grace. "I can see the other kids doing things for Jessica and looking for some recognition or reward. But with Meaghan it was just done naturally."

Rebecca Regan, age 9

The children are quiet in the grade 4F classroom at Sacred Heart school. The mood is tense. Tonya Firth, the teacher, just walked in to find chalk drawings of dogs and cats on the blackboard. Her fifteen students are sitting at their desks.

This private Catholic school in a port city on the Atlantic coast is one of about 200 Sacred Heart schools around the world. Like the others, it is strict. The school expects students to be polite, courteous, and civil. The children wear uniforms: baby-blue blouses, vests, and green and navy kilts for girls; and oxford shirts and navy slacks for boys. Ms. Firth calls to the front one of the boys, whom she suspects made the drawings. Just then Rebecca Regan stands up.

It is Rebecca's first year at this school, so her classmates don't know her very well. The room is silent, and all eyes are on her. What she says next surprises everyone.

"No, Ms. Firth. It wasn't him," she admits. "What I have to say is I did this. It was me."

The teacher is silent.

"Well, aren't you going to punish me?" Rebecca asks.

"No," Ms. Firth answers. "You may go sit down. Your honesty is enough."

Rebecca's confession surprised her teacher, earning Ms. Firth's respect. "Most children would just curl up and go 'Uh hun, un hun,' " Ms. Firth says. "Rebecca's compassion, sincerity, and honesty really struck me. She risked herself to step out and be honest."

Through her honesty, Rebecca also gained the trust of the other students. She showed them that she wouldn't let someone else take the fall for her deed, proving her sense of loyalty. "I didn't want the other people to get in trouble," she says. "Because then they would probably blame me for something next time. This way, you don't get into trouble next time."

Rebecca is a good friend to many different people. Rather than restricting her loyalty to a select few, she works to earn the trust of everyone. By refusing to play favorites, in fact, Rebecca has become a leader. "I have a lot of friends," Rebecca says. "The boys are even my friends."

"The new school was a big adjustment," her mom adds. "I thought she'd have a harder time. Because she's a very compassionate person, she doesn't alienate herself from people. Everyone wants to be her friend."

Rebecca's compassion shines through at the skating rink, as well. Because she took a couple years off from skating, she ended up in a class with younger kids, six- and seven-year-olds. "They fall down a lot so I have to help them up," she says.

Among her many activities, Rebecca sings in a choir led by her mother, Diane Regan. Last year, Diane asked several of her young singers, including Rebecca, to perform in a production of *Jesus Christ Superstar.*

The musical was a lot of fun, and it was a big hit, too. Crowds packed the house every night and gave the performers standing ovations. And while many plays like this are lucky to break even, this one turned a profit.

During rehearsals, Rebecca worked hard to learn her cues, and helped others remember when to come on stage and when to move. Raquel Duffy, who directed the show at St. Matthew's United Church, says Rebecca deserves much of the credit for the play's success. "She wasn't the oldest, but she seemed like the most mature," says Raquel, who is also a professional actor.

Raquel chose Rebecca to be the first person on stage when the curtain lifted, and Rebecca even became a director for the other children. Here, her secret came in handy: she earned respect by making friends. She offered help, but wasn't bossy.

"If kids in the group weren't focused, she would help them, but it wouldn't be a pushy thing," says Raquel. "If someone didn't know quite when to move she would find an appropriate moment to go over to them. She was helping them. Other kids would say, 'Ah, we screwed up!' Rebecca wouldn't take that tack. Even her brother would listen to her."

Performing in front of houses of 500 people was a big thrill— but after closing night, the kids experienced that letdown that everyone who's ever been in a play can remember. You spend weeks and weeks rehearsing with a group, getting to know the others really well. There's the excitement of performing on stage, and then suddenly it's all over, and you feel lost and alone. To relive the thrill of the show, Rebecca had an idea: form a club.

Rebecca goes to choir practice Wednesdays at four o'clock at St. Paul's, a church near her house. At the back of the church is a special little round room with benches inside, a low ceiling, soft lighting, and a piano—a space some call the "Genie in the Bottle" room. Rebecca and her friends—Julia, Marla, Stephanie, Claudia, and Judith—ages seven to nine, get to choir a few minutes early. They sneak into the Genie room for a weekly meeting of their private, girls-only club: the *Jesus Christ Superstar* Club.

"We liked the play so much, we have a club to remember it by," Rebecca explains. The club itself is much like other secret kids' clubs. "We have an assistant," Rebecca says. "Judith's little sister Martha is in grade one. She's too young to be a club member, but she does stuff with us. She gets the markers so we can color. We all hang out all the time."

Forming the club is just yet another example of how Rebecca brings people together. A leader by nature, she has a knack for making and keeping friends. Perhaps this is because she understands the importance of cooperation.

"The other day my friends in the school yard wanted to make snow angels and make a snow fort, so I went along with it. If people want to do something, you do it, and then the next time they want to do something, you can say, 'We want to do this.' I like getting along with people."

Cassandra McPhee, age 12

It's the end of lunchtime on a January day at Lillian Public School. Cassandra McPhee and her friends have gone to their lockers to get their books for their next class. On their way back through the hallway, they see some kids reading a notice taped to the wall. As they get closer, they realize it's the list of people chosen to play on the school basketball team. Cassie, who tried out a few days ago, is anxious to see if she's made the team.

"There was a whole crowd of people," Cassie, then nine, remembers. "Everybody rushed up to the notice. I looked for my name, but it wasn't there. I felt really bad. I was really sad because I like basketball a lot. I thought I was pretty good."

That evening, Cassie cried and cried. Her mom, Cindy, put her arms around her and tried to cheer her up. "As long as you try, you are a winner," she said. "People who don't try things are not winners."

Seeing his daughter cry, Cassie's father, John, went down into the basement and found his old blue and white practice basketball. He plugged a pump into the car lighter and filled the ball with air. He brought the ball upstairs to show Cassie, and after talking, the two made a pact to practice every weekend once the weather warmed. "Every Sunday Mom works so that's our day together," Cassie explains. "We went down to the school yard near our house and spent a couple of hours every Sunday, practicing."

Cassie and her dad practiced all the different moves. They dribbled. They shot baskets from different angles. They threw long balls from the three-point line. They played one on one, did lay ups, and practiced passing the ball. "Then we went down to the corner store where Mom works and got an ice cream or a popsicle," says Cassie, now twelve. She flashes a wide smile, revealing her white teeth.

The next January, Cassie tried out for the basketball team again. "I was feeling pretty well because I thought I had improved lots," she says. Cassie was right to feel more confident. Thanks to her Sunday practices, this time she made the team.

Cassie McPhee is a winner, and not just at basketball. She plays piano, is learning the trumpet, and is also an honors student. Last year, out of sixty children, she won the Principal's Award for Student Leadership. Her secret is her solid relationship with her parents—Cassie's mom and dad are her best friends. They encourage and support her, and she helps them in return.

The McPhees aren't rich. They live in a rented bungalow in the north end of a big, eastern city, and both parents work two jobs. Cassie's mom cleans houses and works in the corner store; her dad works shifts at a packaging factory and stacks shelves at a grocery store. Cassie's Christmas wish was Internet access. She didn't get it, though her parents insist it is coming.

But even if Cassie's parents can't give her all the clothes or stuff that other kids get, they give her their time and encouragement, a kind of support that many wealthier kids go without. "If I get a good mark on my math test, my parents congratulate me," she says. "Other kids' parents will say, 'Oh yeah, whatever,' and even if they had a bad mark they don't ask them where they went wrong or help them to improve.' "

Cassie works at supporting her parents, too. "My parents expect me to be responsible," she says. She is sitting at her kitchen table, eating a ham sandwich her mom made, pausing once in awhile to stroke Ziggy, the big white cat at her feet. "Mummy washes the laundry, then I fold it and put it away. And I set the table every night, and dry the dishes, because we don't have a dishwasher. I also feed the cats."

Life's not always a picnic. Like all families, Cassie and her parents have their moments. Cassie is as stubborn as a mule, and sometimes she clashes with her father. And she has a long-running battle with her mom over the length of her hair. Cassie's mom loves her daughter's long, flowing blond hair and won't allow her to cut it short.

"Mom's hair is too thin for her to wear it this long," says Cassie. "So she's living the long hair she never had through me." Cindy argues that Cassie will appreciate having long hair when she's a teenager, and that she'll thank her for it then. But Cassie disagrees. "When I'm a teenager," she insists,

"I'm going to cut it off."

Still, by and large, Cassie and her folks get along very well. That strong bond gives Cassie the level of self-confidence she needs to succeed in life. And her parents' thoughtfulness and generosity have rubbed off on her. She recently came up with a wonderful idea while reading a book she got from the school library. In *Fruit Flies, Friends, and Fortune Cookies*, by Anne LeMieux, the eleven-year-old heroine, Mary Ellen, throws a bon voyage party for her best friend, who is moving away. Cassie asked her teacher if the class could throw a similar party for her friend Maria. "The teacher thought it was a great idea," says Cassie. "He didn't even know that Maria was moving away."

With her teacher's consent, Cassie went straight to work. On a sheet of loose leaf paper, she wrote a list of things needed for the party: a sign that says, "Farewell, Maria G.," food, chips, pop, bowls, cups, napkins, music, a radio, and tapes. She also wrote: "We could send Maria and Mary to the library for a book. When she and Mary come back in, we could have all the lights turned off and say, 'Surprise!' "

Thanks to her kindness and positive attitude, Cassie makes friends all over the place, impressing her teachers. Cassie's fourth grade teacher, Debbie Attas, hired her at the end of August to sharpen pencils and wash desks in preparation for the new school year. Ms. Attas, who has taught school for nineteen years, is proud of her former student. "Cassie just has a great heart," she says. "She's the kind of citizen you want. She seems to have a great sense of self-assurance. She is willing to take risks, and she is not afraid to ask, 'Can you explain that to me again?' "

"The ones who succeed," continues Ms. Attas, "regardless of wealth or background or heritage, are the ones who have the support of their parents."

Cassie has that support. And she gladly returns it, revealing her sense of loyalty. Sitting in the kitchen, Cassie's father is telling me about his idea for a song-writing business. "Do you play guitar?" I ask. "I dabble but I'm not very good," he replies. "Yes you are," says Cassie to her father. "You helped me write a song that got me an A."

Update

Cassandra McPhee, *now* age 16

Just as she vowed she would, when she reached her teen years Cassandra McPhee got her long blond hair cut off. Where once it flowed down her back, her hair now stops at her shoulders. She was also wearing fake white nails the day I saw her – when she caught me looking at them, she quickly said "From my semi-formal last Thursday."

Aside from that, Cassie at sixteen is much the same as

Cassie at eleven: bubbly, outgoing, happy. She sticks to the same secret, Be a Loyal Friend. That secret has come in especially handy at her first job at 'Toys "R" Us'.

Cassie needed work to save money for a school trip to Italy and France – her first trip on a plane since she was seven. The trip cost $2,600. Her father agreed to pay half. Cassie looked for work, but no one was hiring. Then her friend Anna found a job at the toy store, and recommended Cassie for a job as well.

One Monday in August, Cassie took a bus to the store. "I was scared when I first went in," she said. "I didn't want to make a mistake." She did not. Now she loves her job in the baby department, helping expectant mothers and fathers choose car seats, strollers, high chairs and cribs. "I just fell in love with everybody there."

Making friends is a skill that comes naturally to Cassie. But she is still diligent about it. At night when she closes the store, she leaves notes for the woman on the morning shift: "Good morning, I hope you have a good day." When I saw Cassie, just before Christmas, she talked about the gifts she planned to buy for everyone at the store: a stuffed monkey for one girl, a pair of pajama pants for another.

Cassie is careful, though, not to neglect her studies. "This month has been really heavy with school," she tells me. "I gave away hours because I knew I needed the time to study. I didn't need the money so much anymore." She has already earned all the money she needs for the trip to Europe. That is where the friendships come in handy: Cassie never has trouble finding someone to work her shift. What's more, her friend Anna lives near the shop, so after school Cassie goes there to eat supper before starting work.

At school, Cassie still plans parties. The week before I saw her she'd thrown a party for a teacher who was leaving and for another on her birthday. This involved planning. She passed around a sheet in class for each person to write down what they could bring: chips, cookies, soft drinks, forks, plates, napkins. Cassie herself had planned to be a teacher, but she says, "Now I'm not sure."

Most important of all, she maintains her close friendship with her parents. They just bought her a new cell phone, with a pink leather case. On her phone, Cassie shows me photographs of ... you guessed it. All her friends.

7 Be a Team Player

Courtney Mamakeesic, age 9

Courtney Mamakeesic lives in a remote nothern town. If you take a left turn out of her laneway, drive down the road a bit, and take another left, you come to a sign for the Campbell Mine. For many years, miners have been digging gold out of the ground here. Not far from the mine, there is a recreation center that the company built for the miners and their families. The center includes bowling lanes, a curling rink, and a twenty-five-meter swimming pool.

Courtney is a Native Indian of the Oji-Cree tribe. Born to parents who were too young to raise her, she now lives with her grandparents. Her grandfather isn't a miner; he's Executive Director of a tribal council for Indian reserves that are scattered even farther north. But these days you don't have to be a miner's daughter to swim in the Campbell pool. So, two years ago, Courtney signed up for swimming lessons. Now she is a proud member of the Campbell Goldfins, the mine-sponsored swim team, and competes at swim meets across her region.

"When I was little we used to live by the lake and I used to go swimming there," Courtney says. "Then we moved." Courtney had never swum in a pool before, so she was a bit scared to try it. Luckily, her grandparents encouraged her. "At first I said, 'Hmmm, I don't know,' " Courtney recalls. "But my grandmother said, 'You can learn to swim faster.' " Convinced it might be fun, Courtney decided to take the plunge.

That first day, Courtney had trouble with the breaststroke; she swam with her fingers open. Since then, she has improved quickly. Last year she swam the twenty-five meters in twenty-four seconds; this year she has improved her time, and can swim that same race in eighteen seconds.

"She likes to swim," says her grandfather, Geordi Kakepetum. "That's all she ever wanted to do since she was small. She's a natural swimmer, and she has dedication. She won't miss any practices. She watched the Olympics when swimming was on. She wants to be an Olympic swimmer."

Swim races measure individual speed, so at first glance it would seem this is a very individualistic sport. But Courtney, through her words and actions, proves that this is not so. In fact, she says, team spirit is key to the success of the Goldfins whenever they compete.

"When we're at meets, I'm yelling, I'm like saying, 'Go! Go!' to whoever's racing," says Courtney. "It helps. Whenever they hear someone yell, they go faster, or try to." Courtney adds that it's important to give encouragement after the race, too, even if the swimmer has lost. "I just say, 'Good job, anyway,' even if they came in last place, to make them feel good."

Courtney says the swim team has cemented bonds of friendship between her and other team members. She's become especially close with three little girls named Erin, Gillian, and Katelyn. Courtney calls Katelyn, "My closest friend I ever had."

Good teamwork runs in Courtney's family. Her uncle, Aaron Kakepetum, who is nineteen, is a star hockey player who rose through the system to become the only Native on a junior hockey team in his region. Now Aaron has hockey scholarship offers from Yale and other US schools.

Not all Natives are as successful as this family has been. With their land gone and much of their hunting and trapping culture gone with it, many have trouble finding a new path. A great number of Native children follow their parents into a cycle of alcohol or drug dependency, which has led to high levels of suicide and imprisonment among Native youth. Geordi and Lynda Kakepetum, who are parent figures for both Aaron and Courtney, do not want their children to fall into that trap. They say team sports have helped the kids learn discipline, feel good about themselves, make friends, and gain respect from their peers.

"My son has grown up to be a good young man," Geordi says. "And the sports kept him busy instead of getting into mischief downtown. People in his class looked up to my son as a leader, and that makes it that much easier for us too." Still, according to Geordi, Natives are not always readily accepted. "You have to be twice as good as everyone else to be recognized," he explains.

Athletic success requires another kind of teamwork: cooperation between parent and child. It costs the family a fair bit to pay for Courtney's swim lessons three times a week, plus the trips, plus the goggles that she always seems to be losing in the pool. But Geordi says he doesn't mind spending the money. He and Lynda are willing to support both kids in their activities as long as Courtney and Aaron fulfill their own responsibilities.

"We made a deal with our son when he was very young," says Lynda. "We said 'We'll support you in anything as long as your schoolwork stays good.' He's kept his end of the deal and we've had to keep our end. And I'm sure it's the same thing with Courtney. We'll take her to a swim meet across the country as long as she's doing good in school."

Geordi says his daughter is a team player even when she is not at the swimming pool. "She is pretty considerate. She goes out of her way to make other people feel at ease or comfortable. At home, she helps with cooking and with the dishes." But, alas, "Her room is an absolute mess," says Geordi.

Courtney does her part for the swim team, as well. Last year she swam 120 lengths in two days at the swim-a-thon to raise money for the Goldfins. "We're having another swim-a-thon next Friday," she says. "I'm going to try to do 200 lengths."

Lauren Tannenbaum, age 12

It's a Saturday morning in April. Lauren Tannenbaum and her mother, Shirley, get up at half past six, toss Lauren's violet gym bag from the Winstonettes Gymnastics Club into the minivan, and head off. They pick up Lauren's teammate, Carolyn, and her mother, and then pull onto the highway.

A few weeks earlier, Lauren had a dismal performance at the third qualifier gymnastics meet, and wound up ranking last. "I was crying," she recalls. Today, her mom is driving her to a super-qualifier meet in a city that's a four-hour drive from home. It's Lauren's last chance to make it into the provincial championships. Carolyn has already qualified, but she and her mom are coming to cheer Lauren on.

Everything is going fine, when just a few minutes short of their destination, the minivan dies in a dip in the road. Shirley tries to call a tow truck, but her phone doesn't work. Luckily, Carolyn's mother's phone does.

The towing firm promises to be there soon, but Lauren is already starting to get nervous. The clock is ticking and she doesn't want to be late for her important competition. Not wanting to waste any time, she clambers into the back of the van, slips into her purple and gold gym suit, and pulls her tracksuit on over top. She and Carolyn step outside and pace nervously around the car. The tow truck still hasn't arrived, and Lauren is getting more anxious by the second.

A few minutes later, another car slows and pulls up next to them. Miraculously, a woman driver leans out her window and asks, "Are you going to the gymnastics meet?" Lauren recognizes the woman from other competitions, so her mom allows her to accept the driver's offer for a ride.

Thanks to the support of her family, friends, and the kindness of a woman who rescued her from the side of the road, Lauren not only made it to her competition on time—she qualified very well.

In gymnastics, winners stand alone on the podium. But as Lauren's story shows, it takes a team of supporters to help get them there. Throughout her life, Lauren has worked to be supportive of her club members, and they usually support her back. Along with her parents, her "family" at the gym has been a great source of strength for her.

At the suggestion of a daycare worker, Lauren began gymnastics at age three. "She was climbing everything in sight," recalls Steve, her father. "The daycare worker said, 'You better get this kid into a program where she can try and do this stuff safely.'"

At first Lauren went to gymnastics just once a week. By age nine she had worked her way up to a grueling regimen: she practiced gym four evenings on weekdays and eight hours on Sundays. The pace, and the coach, proved a bit too intense, however, so last year Lauren switched to a new gym. She now trains fifteen hours a week.

"Lauren said, 'Mummy, I want to go to the Winstonettes because the girls are so nice—they're my friends,'" Shirley recalls.

Lauren is happier now, even though her schedule remains very busy. She gets to school at 8:40 a.m., and studies in Hebrew immersion until 11:45 a.m. After lunch, she has general studies from 12:29 p.m. to 4:30 p.m. Then, one of her parents drives her to the gym. She arrives at around five, and squeezes in a bit of homework before beginning three hours of training. She gets home at around nine, eats dinner, finishes her homework, and goes to bed. On average, she does about two hours of homework per night.

"I just like learning and trying new things, I guess, and also I have fun when I do them," says Lauren. "This week I tried giants, where you go around the bar without your legs touching the bar. And I did that on the high bar."

But, for Lauren, the gym is more than just a place to have fun. It is also a mutual support group for her peers. The girls are there to cheer when their friends succeed, and comfort them when they fail. "At third qualifier, Sam wasn't having a good day," recalls Lauren. "She fell on the beam, which was only the second time she'd done that in competition. And she fell on her first tumbling line on the floor. She was crying and I put my arm around her."

"I always find it amazing how they support each other," says Lauren's mother. "They're all competing against each other, and yet they'll still root for one another."

Teamwork has its benefits in all areas of life. When she turned twelve, Lauren celebrated her bat mitzvah, the religious initiation ceremony for Jewish girls. It was a huge affair, and Lauren's whole family helped to make it a success. Her mother decorated the hall with painted masks and balloons, and caterers served food for 250 people. But the showstopper was Lauren herself, who made a speech about teamwork throughout Biblical history. As a gymnast, Lauren had learned to perform with poise and ease. It served her well on that important day. "She spoke incredibly eloquently," recalls Gayle Akler, a friend who attended the bat mitzvah. Lauren's delivery stole the show, and as for the writing, she can thank her father, who is an advertising copywriter.

"Women and men are two separate entities," Lauren told the assembled. "They each fulfill a different function. If one would ask which is more important to a body's survival, a brain or a heart, what would it be? They're both vital. Each organ must do its job to insure the body's survival. So it is with men and women. We each have our role to fulfill."

Graeme Moore, age 9

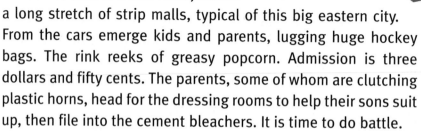

On a bleak Saturday at noon, cars pull into the parking lot of a brick arena. The rink is next to a fast-food joint on a long stretch of strip malls, typical of this big eastern city. From the cars emerge kids and parents, lugging huge hockey bags. The rink reeks of greasy popcorn. Admission is three dollars and fifty cents. The parents, some of whom are clutching plastic horns, head for the dressing rooms to help their sons suit up, then file into the cement bleachers. It is time to do battle.

The tension is high. The winner of this novice game, Parkwood Stars vs. Faustina, advances in the Select league playoffs. Spectators shout and blow their horns as players skate onto the ice. All that equipment sure makes the skaters look like hockey players, but the eight- and nine-year-olds can hardly support the weight of all their gear. It's like watching the Munchkins from *The Wizard of Oz* play hockey in slow motion.

All the action is in the stands. As the Stars' goalie jumps on the puck and a Faustina player tries to dig it out with his hockey stick, the crowd goes wild. "C'mon, ref!" yells Glen Moore, father of Stars defenseman Graeme Moore. "You gotta call that stuff! No pitchforking!" When the referee fails to blow his whistle, Glen bellows, "Okay, ref, you owe us."

By the end of this game, the teams skate to a 0–0 tie. As for Graeme, the game is a major victory for one simple reason: he stayed out of the penalty box. For the Stars' defenseman, this is a big improvement over past games.

Graeme comes from a hockey family. His father, Glen Moore, has played since childhood, and his mother, Carla Reipas, has been fascinated with the game for just as long. "In high school I had the rule book memorized," she says. Glen and Carla's two daughters never played hockey, but Graeme, the youngest, wanted to lace up hockey skates just like Dad.

Some parents put their kids on a hockey rink before they can skate, and the poor little tykes lean on their sticks to keep from falling onto the ice. This wasn't Graeme's case. His mother didn't want to rush him into hockey. "I said, 'He's not taking a stick out there if he can't skate,'" recalls Carla, sitting with Graeme in the kitchen of their home. So Graeme took skating lessons for two years, and played his first hockey game at age seven.

But long before he ever picked up a hockey stick, Graeme received lessons from another source: the National Hockey League. He loved to watch NHL games on television with his sister Kelly and his dad. Week after week, he watched players slash, check, and flatten each other into the boards, occasionally throwing off their gloves for a brawl. So when little Graeme finally got out onto the ice, he thought that was how he was supposed to play.

The young hockey player received all kinds of mixed

messages. On TV, the players whack each other, but in Graeme's league, contact hockey doesn't start until age ten. Slam into another player, and you wind up cooling your skates in the penalty box. Meanwhile, parents scream and swear from the stands, ratcheting up the pressure another notch. By the end of the regular season, the Parkwood Stars had seventy-two penalty minutes, and thirty of them were Graeme's.

One game, Carla recalls, "Graeme fell and slid into the corner and three kids came up and decided they would try to get the puck out. They were all poking him and Graeme got mad." But when Graeme fought back, the referee gave him a penalty and a committee suspended him for one game.

Glen says it was at that point that he decided it was time to talk to his son. "I told him 'Hockey's a team sport,' " he recalls. "I asked, 'How many goals can you score from the penalty box, and how many goals can your team score when they're four against five?' I told him he's got to think of the team when he takes the slash against the guy or punches back."

The talk succeeded, Glen says. "In the last four or five games I don't think he's had a penalty. It's a great tribute to his ability to understand and do what's needed."

"I don't really care if we lose or something," Graeme comments. "It's just a game." He says even the coaches get all riled up sometimes, taking the sport too seriously. But Graeme now understands that the purpose of any sport is to have fun and play as a team.

Graeme has plenty of other pursuits. Arriving home from

school, he says, "Look, Mom, what I found in the library," and pulls a book, *The Hungry Thing Returns*, out of his school bag. Later he's in his room, showing me how he can play "Für Elise" on the electric piano, and I notice a trophy on his table. Turns out, that's nothing. He pulls a cardboard box off a top shelf in his closet, which has "Major awards," written on it in felt pen. There are twenty-eight trophies for T-ball, baseball, softball, hockey, curling, and cross-country running. "They get a lot more awards than when I was a kid," his father jokes, passing by the room.

Despite all the tough talk of hockey and penalties, Graeme remains every inch a kid. His room is full of stuffed penguins and bears, and a well-worn Cat in the Hat and teddy bear rest by his pillow. Hockey and baseball are fine, but he also loves to watch movies in the basement with his parents and sisters. And his sister, Erin, who is sixteen, reads him *Harry Potter* before he goes to sleep.

Graeme credits his strong family for making him a team player. While other parents yell at their kids on the rink or the field, Graeme's just give him support. He appreciates that.

"You're not loud, you and dad," he says to his mom.

Update

Graeme Moore, *now* age 14

Five years ago when I met him, Graeme Moore was not a very good hockey player. Now, at fourteen, he's tall – in the past year alone, he grew half the height of my nine-inch notepad. And today Graeme, who plays defense for the Goulding Park Rangers, is a high-level athlete. When I caught up with him halfway through the season, the Rangers were undefeated after twenty games. In some ways, though, he's still the same Graeme. Remember how he was spending too much time in the penalty box?

"Graeme still takes a few too many penalties," said his coach, Vince Petrielli. "That part hasn't changed."

I caught up with Graeme at home, where his mother, Carla, was giving him cheese, crackers, soup and water as an afternoon snack. I asked him why he gets so many penalties. He shrugged, but his mother knew the answer.

"If someone takes a run at your goalie, you're on him, right?"

"Yeah," shrugged Graeme.

"If someone takes a slash at one of your players, you're on him for the next shift, right?"

"Right," said Graeme.

"You're the protector, you're there for your teammates?"

"Right."

In short, nothing has changed. Graeme still swears by the

same secret. He is a team player.

His team wins thanks to hard work. At a practice I watched, the players, whose warm-up jerseys bear their nick-names, "Frosty" and "Boy Wonder" (Graeme is "Blondy"), skated to the blue line, dropped and rolled twice, got up, skated to the other blue line, dropped and rolled again. As we watched, nearby hockey dad Claude Desjardins, praised Graeme for his good-natured attitude.

"He's a jovial kind of guy," Claude said. "Even though they're playing an intense game, he's got something to say to keep it light. My son sometimes forgets to have fun. And when this is all over, it's the fun that they're going to remember."

Graeme's trademark, when there is a big hit or a big goal, is a full-throated "Whaaat!!" – his imitation of comedian Dave Chappelle making fun of the rapper Lil John.

This fall, Graeme entered a special public high school, the Birchmount Exceptional Athlete Program. To get in, he had to succeed at trials that sound like the tasks of Hercules: fifty-meter dash, zig-zag course around poles, flexed arm hang, standing long jump, and medicine ball toss.

It all may sound rather intense. But Graeme is still a kid. For Christmas, he asked for a flying saucer, to go tobogganing on the hill by his house. Even at hockey, as Graeme has shown, it's not all seriousness. In the changing room, he and his teammates often sit around and gab, rather than put on their equipment. "I go in," said the coach, "and I say, 'Can't you guys, like, maybe email each other later?' "

Get on the path to success with **Lobster Press!**

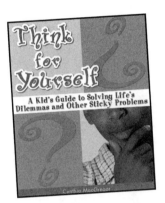